OCCASIONAL PAPER

India's and Pakistan's Strategies in Afghanistan

Implications for the United States and the Region

Larry Hanauer • *Peter Chalk*

CENTER FOR ASIA PACIFIC POLICY

International Programs at RAND

The research described in this report was conducted within the RAND Center for Asia Pacific Policy under the auspices of the International Programs of the RAND Corporation.

Library of Congress Cataloging-in-Publication Data

Hanauer, Larry.
  India's and Pakistan's strategies in Afghanistan : implications for the United States and the region / Larry Hanauer, Peter Chalk.
    p. cm.
  Includes bibliographical references.
  ISBN 978-0-8330-7662-5 (pbk. : alk. paper)
  1. Afghanistan—Foreign relations—India. 2. India—Foreign relations—Afghanistan. 3. Afghanistan—Foreign relations—Pakistan. 4. Pakistan—Foreign relations—Afghanistan. 5. United States—Foreign relations—Afghanistan. 6. United States—Foreign relations—South Asia. I. Chalk, Peter. II. Title.

  DS357.6.I4H36 2012
  327.540581—dc23

                                                                              2012031136

The RAND Corporation is a nonprofit institution that helps improve policy and decisionmaking through research and analysis. RAND's publications do not necessarily reflect the opinions of its research clients and sponsors.

RAND® is a registered trademark.

Published 2012 by the RAND Corporation
1776 Main Street, P.O. Box 2138, Santa Monica, CA 90407-2138
1200 South Hayes Street, Arlington, VA 22202-5050
4570 Fifth Avenue, Suite 600, Pittsburgh, PA 15213-2665
RAND URL: http://www.rand.org/
To order RAND documents or to obtain additional information, contact
Distribution Services: Telephone: (310) 451-7002;
Fax: (310) 451-6915; Email: order@rand.org

Preface

India and Pakistan are both keen to influence developments in Afghanistan, both to advance their own geopolitical, defense, and economic interests and to prevent the other from gaining any advantage. Their competition, however, complicates efforts to place Afghanistan on a sustainable path toward political stability, economic growth, and regional integration.

This report compares Indian and Pakistani interests in Afghanistan and the ways in which each state has sought to further its objectives. It also examines how Kabul navigates the Indian-Pakistani rivalry to protect and advance its own interests. Finally, the paper discusses the implications of the India–Pakistan rivalry for U.S. policy in the region and for U.S. efforts to sustain stability in Afghanistan after the drawdown of combat troops in 2014.

This paper should be of interest to analysts and policymakers concerned with U.S. policy in South Asia and nation-building efforts in Afghanistan, as well as those interested, more broadly, in Indian and Pakistani foreign policy. This research was conducted within the RAND Center for Asia Pacific Policy, part of International Programs at the RAND Corporation. The center aims to improve public policy by providing decisionmakers and the public with rigorous, objective research on critical policy issues affecting Asia and U.S.-Asia relations.

For more information on the RAND Center for Asia Pacific Policy, see http://www.rand.org/international_programs/capp/ or contact the director (contact information is provided on the web page).

Contents

Figures

Summary

India and Pakistan have highly disparate goals for Afghanistan, and they thus undertake very different activities there. Delhi has striven to bolster the government in Kabul and integrate Afghanistan into wider regional political and economic structures. This has not been done out of any sense of altruism. By strengthening Afghanistan, India advances its own national security objectives—namely, eliminating a critical safe haven for terrorists who have attacked India and continue plotting to do so in the future, projecting power throughout South Asia (and beyond), and gaining access to Central Asian trade and energy resources. Although Delhi's goals for Afghanistan certainly involve minimizing Islamabad's influence there, the government's overall policy is geared primarily to advancing India's broader domestic and regional interests independently of its rivalry with Pakistan.

In contrast, Pakistan's goals for Afghanistan are mainly—although not exclusively—India-centric and focus primarily on undermining Delhi's influence in Afghanistan. Islamabad seeks a weak Kabul government dominated by a pliant, supportive Taliban so that Pakistan can maintain "strategic depth" against an Indian invasion, guarantee safe haven for Islamist proxies that it supports, prevent Delhi from projecting power in South Asia, and obstruct India's ability to support separatists in the Pakistani province of Balochistan. In Islamabad's Afghanistan calculus, protecting itself against Indian encroachment takes precedence over pursuing Pakistan's broader geopolitical and economic goals. Part of the reason for this strategic orientation is the preeminent decisionmaking role played by Pakistan's military, which emphasizes security matters over virtually all other elements of foreign policy. So long as India is viewed as an existential threat, and so long as the military plays a central role in setting Pakistani policy, it is unlikely that there will be a fundamental shift in this policy bias.[1]

With its military-dominated decisionmaking apparatus focused on internal security concerns and on keeping other powers from exerting influence in Afghanistan, Pakistan has little of positive value to offer Afghanistan or other countries in the region. Pakistan is not positioned well to boost trade, and it has demonstrated little willingness to take steps designed to improve the lives of ordinary Afghans. By contrast, India's democratic polity, institutionalized decisionmaking processes, relative internal stability, apolitical military, large consumer base, and growing economy make it a far more palatable partner for Kabul. Thus, although Hamid Karzai's government has clearly been prepared to play India and Pakistan against one another—often effectively—it has also taken explicit steps to distance itself from Islamabad while embracing Delhi's cooperation and assistance.

---

[1]   Shahrbanou Tadjbakhsh, *South Asia and Afghanistan: The Robust India-Pakistan Rivalry*, Oslo: Peace Research Institute Oslo, 2011, p. 21–22.

Traditionally, the United States has portrayed its policies in South Asia as aiming to strike a balance between India and Pakistan in recognition that both are important partners (albeit for different reasons). However, since the early days of the George W. Bush administration, Washington has sought to "delink" the two countries on the assumption that India, as a rising power that is capable of both contributing to regional stability and countering growing Chinese influence, could have more to offer over the long term. It was this calculus that led to the conclusion of a U.S.-Indian Strategic Partnership Agreement in 2004 and a supplemental accord the following year that codified U.S. assistance to India's civilian nuclear sector.[2]

Despite this preference, there is no doubt that Washington has become increasingly dependent on Pakistan's cooperation to combat the near-term threat of Islamic extremism for which, over the past 11 years, it has provided Pakistan with some $16 billion in security-related assistance. The importance of Islamabad's counterterrorism cooperation, as well as its assistance to the Afghan war effort, has driven the United States to accommodate Pakistani sensitivities by encouraging India to remain on the sidelines of international efforts in Afghanistan. With the dual threat of al Qaeda and the Taliban high on the U.S. agenda and a large U.S./North Atlantic Treaty Organization (NATO) force in Afghanistan, whatever additional contributions that India could make to Afghan security and reconstruction have been seen as less critical to U.S. policy in Afghanistan than ensuring Islamabad's continued partnership.

That said, U.S. courting of Pakistan—whether through the provision of billions of dollars in U.S. aid or past commitments to minimize Indian involvement in Afghanistan—has so far failed to reduce Pakistan's support for militancy and terrorism, and there is no reason to think that this will change. Washington has repeatedly learned that it cannot rely on Islamabad to rein in militants whom the Pakistani military sees as valuable strategic assets in countering Indian power and influence—one of the reasons the United States has come to rely increasingly on unilateral operations to combat terrorists.

In addition to backing insurgents who have repeatedly attacked coalition forces in Afghanistan,[3] Islamabad has undermined Washington's efforts to negotiate a political settlement with the Taliban, which is seen as critical to securing the eventual withdrawal of U.S. combat troops; obstructed shipments of military materiel to U.S. and NATO forces by closing its borders to such cargo; refused to investigate how Osama bin Laden managed to hide in the country for so many years without being detected; pledged to increase purchases of Iranian oil despite international sanctions on Tehran; and allowed Chinese officials to examine the wreckage of a U.S. helicopter that crashed during the raid on the al Qaeda leader's compound in Abbottabad.[4]

By early 2012, Pakistan's repeated, deliberate efforts to undercut U.S. policies had clearly prompted U.S. officials to reconsider the value of the overall security partnership with Islamabad. This became clear when Secretary of Defense Leon Panetta, during a June 2012 trip to Afghanistan and India, issued Washington's starkest criticism yet of Pakistan, pointedly stat-

---

[2]   Ashley J. Tellis, "The Merits of Dehyphenation: Explaining U.S. Success in Engaging India and Pakistan," *Washington Quarterly*, Vol. 31, No. 4, Autumn 2008, pp. 30–32, 36.

[3]   For details on one such attack, see David S. Cloud and Alex Rodriguez, "CIA Gets Nod to Step Up Drone Strikes in Pakistan," *Los Angeles Times*, June 8, 2012.

[4]   Anna Fifield, "Pakistan Lets China See US Helicopter," *Financial Times*, August 14, 2011.

ing that Washington was "reaching the limits of [its] patience" with Islamabad's refusal to crack down on terrorist safe havens operating in its territory.[5]

Panetta further noted India's positive contributions to Afghanistan's economic and commercial development and, arguably more significantly, expressed support for Delhi's training of the country's nascent armed forces and encouraged it to continue with this security assistance mission. Panetta's implicit nod to Indian military engagement in Afghanistan represented a significant shift in U.S. policy away from Pakistan and an acknowledgment that Delhi had more to offer in terms of promoting Afghanistan's internal stability.

As the United States prepares to draw down its military presence in Afghanistan, it will become less dependent on Pakistan to transport military materiel or to undertake efforts to rein in extremist attacks on U.S. troops. At the same time, Washington will seek to ensure that its departure does not leave a security vacuum or a break in reconstruction efforts. To help prevent such developments, Washington could promote a proactive Indian role in Afghanistan—particularly in the security sector—as a means of fostering internal and regional stability and as a way to preserve and build on U.S. achievements in Afghanistan. Doing so would require U.S. policymakers to once again delink U.S. policies toward India and Pakistan to take advantage of the long-term strategic benefits of partnering with India.

Greater Indian involvement in Afghanistan will promote objectives that both the United States and India share. Indian political mediation and training for the Afghan military and police can help avert violence and internal conflict. At the same time, Delhi's interactions with the Kabul government—which have involved all Afghan ethnic groups to some degree, despite India's history of support for Tajiks, Uzbeks, and other non-Pashtuns—will help marginalize the Taliban and the extremist groups that target both India and the United States. Just as importantly, India's continued development aid can contribute to improvements in health care, education, power generation, and other critical sectors, and its extensive private investment and efforts to integrate Afghanistan into regional trade arrangements will promote the type of economic growth that is critical for the country's long-term stability.

A robust Indian role in Afghanistan should serve to advance other U.S. foreign policy objectives as well. In its efforts to gain greater access to Central Asian energy markets, for example, Delhi will need to develop an effective trade and transportation infrastructure in Afghanistan to connect with the Central Asian Republics (CARs), particularly Turkmenistan, Uzbekistan, and Kazakhstan. This will, in turn, reduce China's influence in South and Central Asia—an objective that both Washington and Delhi share. Furthermore, as India increasingly aspires to be a dominant regional actor, its contributions will help reduce the level of U.S. involvement and resources needed to stabilize that part of the world. Supporting a more robust role for Delhi—which would contribute to Afghanistan's security, stability, and economic development—is thus a more effective long-term strategy for both countering terrorism and stabilizing Afghanistan than continuing to partner with Pakistan on short-term counterterrorism operations.

Because Islamabad would vociferously oppose both an increasingly robust Indian presence in Afghanistan and U.S. support for such a role, Pakistan would likely respond in ways detrimental to both Indian and U.S. interests. It could, for instance, retaliate against India

---

[5] Jim Garamone, "U.S. Reaching Limit of Patience with Pakistan on Safe Havens," *American Forces Press Service*, June 7, 2012.

with political, economic, and military pressure while moving to hinder U.S. military operations in Afghanistan and undermine U.S. counterterrorism efforts.

However, Islamabad's actual retaliatory options are not likely to be very effective at influencing U.S. or Indian policies. Pakistan's cooperation on counterterrorism is already only half-hearted at best; it takes action only against groups that are seen to pose a domestic threat while supporting such entities as the Haqqani network and Lashkar-e-Taiba (LeT). The recently signed U.S.–Afghanistan Strategic Partnership Agreement gives the United States the ability to continue using Afghan territory to pursue al Qaeda and Taliban militants, which would enable U.S. forces to launch attacks on militants' bases in the Federally Administered Tribal Areas (FATA). In addition, because a long-established theme of Pakistani foreign and security policy has been to use jihadi proxies to offset Delhi's political, demographic, and military superiority, it is conceivable that the Indian public would not necessarily link a future terrorist attack to changes in the government's Afghan policy. As such, it is questionable whether the specter of (Pakistani-backed) retributive extremist strikes would actually deter India from pursuing its regional economic and political interests. To be sure, the potential costs associated with enhancing India's profile in Afghanistan must be considered and weighed against the benefits of any such move. However, the drawbacks of withholding Indian assistance simply for fear of eliciting a negative reaction from Islamabad are arguably greater than the pain Pakistan could inflict on either Washington or Delhi through its response.

Should India determine that it can best advance its regional interests by playing a more robust role in Afghanistan, its government would have a spectrum of options available to it. These include, in order of increasing assertiveness, boosting development assistance and investment; deploying additional paramilitary forces to protect Indian diplomats, aid workers, and infrastructure projects; continuing to provide limited military training to the Afghan National Security Forces (ANSF) in India; expanding the types and extent of security assistance provided; conducting military and police training inside Afghanistan; and deploying combat troops to conduct counterterrorism and counterinsurgency (COIN) missions. Of these, the first and last choices would be least preferable. Many Indians already seem to have concluded that years of development assistance alone have not helped to significantly advance India's regional interests, while the deployment of Indian combat troops to Afghanistan would serve as an extreme and very visible provocation of Pakistan. Delhi's most likely course of action would therefore be more attenuated, focusing on increased trade and investment and on instituting moderately assertive protective and security assistance measures. At the same time, India would probably seek to reestablish contacts with leaders of Afghanistan's Tajik and Uzbek communities, as well as build ties with less extreme Taliban figures, as a way of expanding its options for its future bilateral relationship with Kabul.

In sum, not only does Delhi have more to offer than Islamabad to the security and prosperity of South and Central Asia, but its assistance to the ANSF—combined with an increasingly proactive role in fostering and safeguarding Afghan economic and commercial development—also provides the best hope for advancing both U.S. and Indian regional interests. As the United States prepares to withdraw its combat forces from Afghanistan in 2014, it should therefore encourage India to fill any potential security vacuum that might thereby arise by adopting a more robust political, economic, and security stance toward Kabul.

Acknowledgments

We take full responsibility for the views expressed herein, but we wish to express our appreciation for the valuable insights offered by Ashley J. Tellis of the Carnegie Endowment for International Peace and by Jonah Blank and Michael Lostumbo of the RAND Corporation. Their thoughtful suggestions immeasurably improved the arguments and analyses made in this report.

We are also extremely grateful to the RAND Center for Asia Pacific Policy, which provided funding for this research. Without the support of the center and its leadership, this paper would not have been possible.

Abbreviations

ANSF	Afghan National Security Forces
APTTA	Afghanistan–Pakistan Transit Trade Agreement
bcm/y	billion cubic meters per year
BRO	Border Roads Organization
CAR	Central Asian Republic
CBR	Central Board of Revenue
COIN	counterinsurgency
CTF	Combined Task Force
DNI	Director of National Intelligence
EC	European Commission
EU	European Union
FATA	Federally Administered Tribal Areas
GDP	gross domestic product
HuM	Harakat-ul-Mujahideen
IEA	Islamic Emirate of Afghanistan
IMU	Islamic Movement of Uzbekistan
ISI	Inter-Services Intelligence
ITBP	Indo-Tibetan Border Police
JeM	Jaish-e-Mohammed
JUI	Jamiat Ulema-e-Islam
KPK	Khyber Pakhtunkhwa
LeT	Lashkar-e-Taiba
NA	Northern Alliance

NATO	North Atlantic Treaty Organization
NDN	Northern Distribution Network
NWFP	North-West Frontier Province
PRIO	Peace Research Institute Oslo
QST	Quetta Shura Taliban
RAW	Research and Analysis Wing
SAARC	South Asian Association for Regional Cooperation
TAPI	Turkmenistan-Afghanistan-Pakistan-India
TTP	Tehrik-e-Taliban Pakistan
UN	United Nations
UTO	United Tajik Opposition

CHAPTER ONE

Introduction

The tensions between India and Pakistan have significantly shaped events in South Asia since the two countries became independent from Britain in 1947. The countries have fought three wars since then, and the prospect of future conflict drove each of the two nations to develop nuclear weapons to deter the other from contemplating acts of aggression. Pakistan sees India as its primary national security threat even as internal instability appears increasingly likely to lead to the state's collapse. The Indian security apparatus is on constant alert for attacks on its territory by Pakistani-backed extremists, even though the Indian government—whose geopolitical aspirations have grown along with the country's economy—has increasingly come to view China as its primary rival.

Since the withdrawal of Soviet forces from Afghanistan in 1980—and particularly since the fall of the Taliban regime in 2001—both India and Pakistan have injected their conflict into Afghan affairs. Each perceives influence in Afghanistan as critical to achieving its primary national security objectives (though for different reasons), and both approach Afghanistan as a zero-sum dynamic in which one side's gain is a loss for the other. Though present-day Afghanistan is far weaker than its two neighbors, it is not a passive actor; President Hamid Karzai has skillfully attempted to balance the two as he simultaneously works to consolidate control over the country.

Once the United States ends its combat mission in Afghanistan—a step currently anticipated to take place in 2014, though the U.S.–Afghanistan Strategic Partnership Agreement envisions the potential presence of U.S. troops beyond that date—the India-Pakistan rivalry will continue to affect developments in Afghanistan. However, if the two countries continue working to manipulate Afghan affairs so as to advance their own parochial interests, it will be extremely difficult (if not impossible) for Afghanistan to achieve a measure of stability.

India and Pakistan have highly disparate goals for Afghanistan, and they thus undertake very different activities there. Delhi has striven to bolster the government in Kabul and integrate Afghanistan into wider regional political and economic structures. This has not been done out of any sense of altruism. By strengthening Afghanistan, India advances its own national security objectives—namely, eliminating a critical safe haven for terrorists who have attacked India and continue plotting to do so in the future, projecting power throughout South Asia (and beyond), and gaining access to Central Asian trade and energy resources. Although Delhi's goals for Afghanistan certainly involve minimizing Islamabad's influence in the country, Indian policy toward Afghanistan endeavors primarily to advance India's broader domestic and regional interests independently of its rivalry with Pakistan.

In contrast, Pakistan's goals for Afghanistan are mainly India-centric. Islamabad seeks a weak Kabul government dominated by a pliant, supportive Taliban so that it can maintain "strategic depth" against an Indian invasion, guarantee safe haven for anti-Indian proxies, undermine Delhi's influence in Afghanistan, prevent Indian power projection in the broader South/Central Asia region, and obstruct India's ability to support separatists in the Pakistani province of Balochistan. In Islamabad's Afghanistan calculus, protecting Pakistan against Indian encroachment takes precedence over pursuing Pakistan's broader geopolitical and economic goals. Part of the reason for this strategic orientation is the preeminent decisionmaking role played by the Pakistani military, which emphasizes security matters over virtually all other elements of foreign policy. So long as India is viewed as an existential threat, and so long as the military plays a central role in setting Pakistani policy, it is unlikely that there will be a fundamental shift in this policy bias.[1]

Although Pakistan undoubtedly views much of its Afghan strategy through an India-centric prism, it would be wrong to suggest that Islamabad has no other interests or objectives that are relevant to the country. Among the more important are the following:

- ensuring that developments in Afghanistan do not lead to the emergence of a "Pashtuni-stan" straddling both countries or otherwise give rise to unrest and instability in the Federally Administered Tribal Areas (FATA), parts of Balochistan or Khyber Pakhtunkhwa (KPK, formerly known as the North-West Frontier Province, or NWFP)
- related to the above, enforcing the sanctity of the Durand Line—the disputed boundary line between Pakistan and Afghanistan that no Afghan government has ever accepted—to mitigate the spread of Pashtun nationalism in the KPK[2]
- establishing Afghanistan as a conduit for enhancing trade, transportation, and commercial links with the Central Asian Republics (CARs)
- curbing Iranian influence in Afghanistan, which Tehran could use as a forward base from which to launch Shi'a militias into Balochistan
- stemming greater Russian involvement in Afghan affairs, which, given the historical context of the anti-Soviet jihad during the 1980s, Pakistan's security community is unlikely to see as neutral, much less beneficial[3]
- limiting U.S. efforts at brokering peace between Kabul and the Taliban, which many in Islamabad believe would come at the direct expense of Pakistan's strategic interests.

With its military-dominated decisionmaking apparatus focused on internal security concerns and on keeping other powers from exerting influence in Afghanistan, Pakistan has little of positive value to offer either Afghanistan or its neighbors. Pakistan is not positioned well to boost trade, and it has demonstrated little willingness to take steps designed to improve the lives of ordinary Afghans. In contrast, India's democratic polity, institutionalized decision-making processes, relative internal stability, apolitical military, large consumer base, and growing economy make it a far more palatable partner for Kabul.

---

[1] Shahrbanou Tadjbakhsh, *South Asia and Afghanistan: The Robust India-Pakistan Rivalry*, Oslo: Peace Research Institute Oslo, 2011, pp. 21–22.

[2] See, for instance, Ahmed Rashid, *Taliban: Militant Islam, Oil and Fundamentalism in Central Asia*, New Haven, Conn.: Yale University Press, 2010, p. 187.

[3] Many within the Inter-Services Intelligence (ISI) Directorate started their careers as mujahideen trainers and liaison officers, while Moscow (together with India) was one of the main backers of the Tajik-, Uzbek-, and Hazara-dominated Northern Alliance (NA) during the 1990s.

For their part, Afghans are likely to welcome greater Indian involvement in Afghan affairs but oppose further engagement by Pakistan. The Karzai government has played India and Pakistan against each other effectively, but it has taken clear steps to distance itself from Islamabad while embracing Indian cooperation and assistance. Nationwide, Afghan public opinion is extremely hostile toward Pakistan and relatively positive toward India. A 2009 BBC/ABC News/ARD poll found that, although only 8 percent of Afghans held a favorable view of Pakistan, 74 percent of Afghans viewed India favorably. Similarly, although 86 percent thought that Pakistan had a negative influence in Afghanistan (with only 5 percent saying Pakistan made positive contributions), India's impact was seen as positive by 41 percent of Afghans and negative by only 10 percent.[4]

U.S. Policy in South Asia

The United States frequently portrays its policies in South Asia as striking a balance between its two close partners in Delhi and Islamabad. That said, since the early days of the George W. Bush administration, Washington has delinked the two countries and concluded that India, as a rising power capable of contributing to regional stability and countering growing Chinese influence, has more to offer over the long-term—a calculus that led to the 2004 strategic partnership agreement and the U.S. agreement in 2005 to provide assistance to India's civilian nuclear sector.[5] At the same time, however, Washington became increasingly dependent on Pakistan's cooperation to combat the near-term threat of Islamic extremism.

U.S.-Pakistani cooperation on counterterrorism is extensive, and—given the existence of terrorist safe havens on the Pakistani side of the Afghan border—critical to U.S. counterterrorism efforts. Pakistan has assisted in the capture of many al Qaeda operatives and conducted military operations against extremists.[6] It has deployed troops and Frontier Corps paramilitary units along the Afghan border and throughout the tribal areas.[7] Pakistan has also shared a great deal of terrorism-related intelligence with the United States, including a lead that ultimately enabled the U.S. intelligence community to locate Osama bin Laden.[8] In return for this cooperation, and to encourage Islamabad to continue working with Washington, the United States has provided Pakistan with some $16 billion in security-related assistance since

---

[4]   Jill McGivering, "Afghan People 'Losing Confidence,'" BBC News, February 9, 2009.

[5]   Ashley J. Tellis, "The Merits of Dehyphenation: Explaining U.S. Success in Engaging India and Pakistan," *Washington Quarterly*, Vol. 31, No. 4, Autumn 2008, pp. 30–32, 36. Barack Obama's administration has relinked them to some degree, arguing that improved Indian-Pakistani relations would make Pakistan feel sufficiently secure that it would not need to support the Taliban or anti-Indian insurgents to the same degree, though little progress has been made in this regard. See C. Raja Mohan, "How Obama Can Get South Asia Right," *Washington Quarterly*, Vol. 32, No. 2, April 2009, pp. 174–175.

[6]   C. Christine Fair, "2014 and Beyond: U.S. Policy Towards Afghanistan and Pakistan, Part I," testimony before the U.S. House of Representatives Committee on Foreign Affairs Subcommittee on the Middle East and South Asia, November 3, 2011b, p. 43.

[7]   Sherry Rehman, "Ambassador Rehman's Speech at the United States Institute of Peace (USIP)," Washington, D.C., February 15, 2012.

[8]   Devin Dwyer, "Osama Bin Laden Killing: Pakistan Reacts Cautiously to U.S. Raid on Its Soil," ABC News, May 2, 2011.

2001.[9] On March 18, 2011, Secretary of State Hillary Clinton certified to Congress, in accordance with the Enhanced Partnership with Pakistan Act, that Pakistan had made significant efforts to combat terrorism during the previous fiscal year.[10]

The importance of Pakistan's counterterrorism cooperation and assistance to the Afghan war effort drove Washington to accommodate Pakistani sensitivities by encouraging India to remain on the sidelines of international efforts in Afghanistan. With the threat of al Qaeda and the Taliban high on Washington's agenda and a large U.S./North Atlantic Treaty Organization (NATO) force in Afghanistan, whatever additional contributions that India could make to Afghan security and reconstruction were clearly seen as less critical to U.S. policy in Afghanistan than ensuring Pakistan's continued partnership.

Despite accommodating Pakistani concerns and providing the country with massive infusions of U.S. aid, Islamabad has proven to be somewhat of a fair-weather friend. The government has repeatedly cut off U.S. supply routes to Afghanistan, supported militants who attack U.S. troops there, and dedicated significant amounts of U.S. aid to bolster its defenses along the Indian border rather than to combat extremists in the northwest. As a Council on Foreign Relations/Aspen Institute India joint report asserted,

> Instead of a true partnership, the bilateral [U.S.–Pakistan] relationship has degenerated into occasionally positive rhetoric overlaying a transactional relationship in which Pakistan leases access to bases and land routes into Afghanistan in exchange for massive quantities of U.S. aid.[11]

This dynamic, according to Stanford University professor and former State Department official Stephen Krasner,

> is not working. Any gains the United States has bought with its aid and engagement have come at an extremely high price and have been more than offset by Pakistan's nuclear proliferation and its support for the groups that attack Americans, Afghans, Indians, and others.[12]

By early 2012, it was apparent that Pakistan's ongoing efforts to undermine U.S. policies had prompted U.S. officials to reconsider the value of the security partnership with Islamabad. Insurgents tied to Pakistan's ISI Directorate had repeatedly attacked coalition forces in

---

[9]   K. Alan Kronstadt, *Pakistan–U.S. Relations*, Washington, D.C.: Congressional Research Service, R41832, May 24, 2012, p. 38. The $16 billion figure includes actual appropriated amounts for fiscal years 2002–2010 and estimated appropriations for fiscal years 2011 ($1.301 billion) and 2012 ($1.603 billion). Of this, the administration suspended $800 million in July 2011. See "U.S. Suspends $800 Million in Aid to Pakistan," NPR, July 10, 2011.

[10] See Hillary Clinton, Secretary of State, "Certification Relating to Pakistan Under Section 203 of the Enhanced Partnership with Pakistan Act of 2009 (P.L. 111-73)," March 18, 2011, in Jacquelyn L. Williams-Bridgers, *Pakistan Assistance: Relatively Little of the $3 Billion in Requested Assistance Is Subject to State's Certification of Pakistan's Progress on Nonproliferation and Counterterrorism Issues*, Washington, D.C.: U.S. Government Accountability Office, GAO-11-786R, July 19, 2011a, p. 10.

[11] Christopher Clary, *The United States and India: A Shared Strategic Future*, New York: Council on Foreign Relations Press, 2011, p. 13.

[12] Stephen D. Krasner, "Talking Tough to Pakistan," *Foreign Affairs*, January–February 2012.

Afghanistan and assaulted the U.S. embassy in Kabul last September.[13] Islamabad has undermined Washington's efforts to negotiate a political settlement with the Taliban—seen as critical to securing the eventual withdrawal of U.S. combat troops—by detaining and, many believe, assassinating members of the group who are inclined to compromise.[14] The government had refused to investigate how Osama bin Laden managed to hide in the country for so many years without being detected, and it recently sentenced a local doctor who helped the United States locate bin Laden to 33 years in prison.[15] Finally, Pakistani authorities reportedly allowed Chinese officials to examine the wreckage of a U.S. helicopter that crashed during the raid on the al Qaeda leader's compound in Abbottabad, despite a specific request from the Obama administration to not do so.[16]

During a June 2012 trip to Afghanistan and India, Secretary of Defense Leon Panetta issued the U.S. government's starkest criticism yet of Islamabad, stating that Washington was "reaching the limits of [its] patience" with Islamabad and its refusal to crack down on terrorist safe havens in its territory.[17] Panetta further noted India's positive contributions to Afghanistan's economic and commercial development and, more significantly, expressed support for Delhi's training of the country's nascent armed forces and encouraged it to continue with this security assistance mission. Panetta's nod to Indian military engagement in Afghanistan represented a significant shift in U.S. policy away from Pakistan and an acknowledgment that Delhi could contribute significantly to Afghanistan's internal stability.

Several factors have freed Washington to solicit more active Indian participation in shaping Afghanistan's political and economic future. Certainly, U.S. officials' frustration with Pakistan has led them to question the value of continued bilateral security cooperation. Moreover, as the United States and NATO prepare to draw down their military presence in Afghanistan, they will become less dependent on Pakistan to transport military materiel or rein in Taliban attacks on their troops.

Equally important, however, is the fact that alternatives to Pakistani assistance have become increasingly viable. For instance, when Islamabad closed its borders to NATO supplies headed for Afghanistan (in retaliation for President Obama's refusal to apologize for attacking a Pakistani border post in November 2011), Washington adjusted by firming up agreements with Russia and several Central Asian Republics to move supplies through their territory instead. The United States also secured agreements from these countries to allow the reverse transit of materiel, thereby reducing the need for Pakistani transit routes to ship enormous amounts of equipment out of Afghanistan when U.S. and NATO forces draw down in 2014.

Washington will seek to ensure that the departure of large numbers of coalition forces does not leave a security vacuum or cause a break in reconstruction efforts. Promoting a proactive role for India in Afghanistan could be integral in this regard, both as a means of foster-

---

[13] For details on one insurgent attack, see David S. Cloud and Alex Rodriguez, "CIA Gets Nod to Step Up Drone Strikes in Pakistan," *Los Angeles Times*, June 8, 2012. Regarding the embassy attack, see "Pakistan 'Backed Haqqani Attack on Kabul'—Mike Mullen," BBC News, September 22, 2011.

[14] Thomas Ruttig, "The Taliban Arrest Wave in Pakistan: Reasserting Strategic Depth?" *CTC Sentinel*, Vol. 3, No. 3, March 2010, pp. 5–6; "Taliban Flags Start to Spring Fighting Season," Associated Press, May 2, 2011.

[15] Ismail Khan, "Prison Term for Helping C.I.A. Find bin Laden," *New York Times*, May 23, 2012.

[16] Anna Fifield, "Pakistan Lets China See US Helicopter," *Financial Times*, August 14, 2011.

[17] Jim Garamone, "U.S. Reaching Limit of Patience with Pakistan on Safe Havens," American Forces Press Service, June 7, 2012.

ing internal and regional stability and as a way to preserve and build upon U.S. achievements in the country. Doing so would require U.S. policymakers once again to delink U.S. policies toward India and Pakistan to take advantage of the long-term strategic benefits of partnering with India.

In the near term, such a strategy could alienate Pakistan, thereby hindering U.S. counterterrorism efforts and complicating logistics support to U.S. troops in Afghanistan, both of which rely heavily on Pakistani support. However, the benefits of Pakistani counterterrorism cooperation are limited given Islamabad's simultaneous support for the Taliban and other extremist groups. Furthermore, although transportation costs will be higher, U.S. troops in Afghanistan can be supported through the use of alternate supply routes, and, once U.S. troops are withdrawn or drawn down significantly, Washington will no longer depend as heavily on Pakistani logistics support.

Arguably more complex is India's policymaking calculus. Although Delhi has much to gain by increasing its involvement in Afghanistan, not least in terms of regional power projection, it is not at all clear whether the government would want to assume the roles that the United States is relinquishing in Afghanistan. Not only would such an effort require large amounts of money and manpower, it may also inspire Islamabad—which would almost certainly view increasing Indian influence in Afghanistan as a strategic defeat—to strike back at India as a result.[18] The commander of NATO's International Security Assistance Force and U.S. Forces–Afghanistan, General Stanley A. McChrystal, made this precise point in August 2009: "While Indian activities largely benefit the Afghan people, increasing Indian influence in Afghanistan is likely to exacerbate regional tensions and encourage Pakistani countermeasures in Afghanistan or India."

To offset such concerns, the United States will need to stress to Delhi how an increased role in Afghanistan will be of benefit to all three countries. By providing military and police training and maintaining its close relationship with the Karzai administration, India will help foster internal stability and marginalize the Taliban and other extremist groups that target India (as well as the United States). By promoting bilateral and regional trade, encouraging private investment, and contributing development aid, India will boost its own economy while also facilitating Afghanistan's integration into regional political and economic structures and promoting the type of economic growth that is critical for Afghanistan's long-term stability.

Carving out a robust Indian role in Afghanistan—and convincing Delhi that this would be in its own interest—will serve to advance fundamental U.S. foreign policy objectives in South and Central Asia. In addition to contributing to internal political stabilization (which will have a direct positive impact on regional security), Delhi's efforts to gain greater access to Central Asian energy markets will necessarily require it to develop an effective trade and transportation infrastructure in Afghanistan. This will not only contribute to Kabul's further development; more importantly, it will also serve to reduce China's influence in South and Central Asia—an objective that both Washington and Delhi share.[19] Furthermore, as India increasingly aspires to be a dominant regional actor,[20] its contributions will help reduce the

---

[18] Stanley A. McChrystal, commander, International Security Assistance Force and U.S. Forces–Afghanistan, "COMISAF's Initial Assessment," memorandum to Secretary of Defense Robert M. Gates, August 30, 2009, p. 2-11.

[19] Harsh V. Pant, "India in Afghanistan: A Test Case for a Rising Power," *Contemporary South Asia*, Vol. 18, No. 2, 2010a, p. 147.

[20] Tadjbakhsh, 2011, pp. vii, 6.

level of U.S. involvement and resources needed to stabilize that part of the world. Supporting a more robust role for Delhi—which would contribute to Afghanistan's security, stability, and economic development—is thus a more effective long-term strategy for both countering terrorism and stabilizing Afghanistan than continuing to partner with Pakistan on short-term counterterrorism operations.

Thus, for the United States, the benefits to be gained from a robust Indian role in Afghanistan far exceed the benefits of continued collaboration with Pakistan on counterterrorism. Washington's relations with Islamabad are already poor and getting worse—the *Atlantic's* December 2011 cover story referred to Pakistan as the "ally from hell"[21]—and the United States would lose few truly significant advantages if ties deteriorate further. Moreover, the United States seems to have little ability to encourage more productive Pakistani behavior, and exasperation appears to be growing among senior U.S. officials that "the terror state we call our ally"[22] continually impedes U.S. counterterrorism objectives and the achievement of U.S. goals in Afghanistan.

Weighing Pakistan's Likely Responses

Pakistan would vociferously oppose both an increasingly robust Indian role in Afghanistan and U.S. support for such a role, and it would likely respond in ways detrimental to both Indian and U.S. interests.

Pakistan could retaliate against India with political, economic, and military pressure by taking one or more of the following steps:

- blocking Afghan exports to India, most of which currently cross Pakistani territory
- pulling out of an arrangement to construct a regional pipeline that would transport natural gas from Turkmenistan to Afghanistan, Pakistan, and India and continue pursuing a bilateral pipeline with Iran in its place
- turning increasingly to China for assistance with military, commercial, and infrastructure development assistance, which could further impede Indian initiatives to project power in South and Central Asia, provide additional military capabilities that could be used against India in an armed conflict, and frustrate Indian efforts to counter Chinese influence in the region
- most critically, encouraging attacks on Indian interests in Afghanistan, escalating insurgent activity in Kashmir, or supporting Mumbai-style terrorist attacks, any one of which would cause a steady stream of Indian casualties and generate significant domestic political turmoil in India.

Pakistan could also take steps that hinder U.S. military operations in Afghanistan and undermine U.S. counterterrorism efforts:

- Pakistan could provide even greater support for the Afghan insurgency than its current provision of safe-haven and operational assistance to the Taliban.

---

[21] Jeffrey Goldberg and Marc Ambinder, "The Ally from Hell," *Atlantic*, December 2011.

[22] Michael Hirsh, "Pakistan: The Terror State We Call Our Ally," *Atlantic*, May 25, 2012, pp. 13–17.

- Islamabad could continue to block supply convoys en route to U.S. troops in Afghanistan from passing through its territory, as it has done several times before. Although Washington has announced that it aims to cease combat missions in Afghanistan by 2014, the United States will almost certainly maintain some troop presence well past this point, both to train the Afghan National Security Forces (ANSF) and to conduct counterterrorism operations. (Both missions are permitted under the U.S.-Afghanistan Strategic Partnership Agreement signed in May 2012.[23]) A long-term prohibition on shipping supplies across Pakistani territory could complicate U.S. logistics efforts, particularly those supporting the withdrawal of U.S. combat forces and materiel from Afghanistan; the United States would be dependent on the longer, more costly, multi-nation Northern Distribution Network (NDN).

- Islamabad could retaliate by withholding counterterrorism assistance, particularly regarding Taliban and al Qaeda fighters and facilitators finding safe haven inside Pakistani territory. To date, however, such cooperation has been inconsistent and unreliable anyway.

These costs are not insignificant, and they must be considered before enhancing India's profile in Afghanistan. However, the costs of withholding Indian assistance for fear of eliciting a negative response from Islamabad are arguably higher. Courting Pakistan—whether through the provision of billions of dollars in U.S. aid or past commitments to minimize Indian involvement in Afghanistan—have not reduced Pakistan's support for militancy and terrorism.[24] Simply put, Washington has repeatedly learned that it cannot rely on Islamabad to rein in militants whom the Pakistani military sees as valuable strategic assets in countering Indian power and influence—one of the reasons the United States has come to rely increasingly on unilateral operations to combat terrorists.

Delhi should be amenable to playing a more active role in Afghanistan, in part because it certainly does not want the U.S. military drawdown to create a vacuum that enables extremists to regroup. As one Indian scholar observes, "The war in Afghanistan is crucial from the point of view of Indian national security. If the Americans withdraw and jihadists emerge with a sense of triumphalism, India will face increasing onslaughts of terrorism."[25] Assuming that the Indian government is willing to become increasingly involved in Afghanistan, Indian policymakers will have to craft a role that advances Indian interests in both Afghanistan and the region without antagonizing Pakistan to such a degree that the latter feels compelled to respond in unproductive ways.

---

[23] Enduring Strategic Partnership Agreement Between the United States of America and the Islamic Republic of Afghanistan, Kabul, May 24, 2012, ¶ III(6).

[24] See, for instance, C. Christine Fair and Peter Chalk, *Fortifying Pakistan: The Role of US Internal Security Assistance*, Washington, D.C.: U.S. Institute of Peace, 2006, pp. 67–69; and Lydia Polgreen and Souad Mekhennet, "Militant Network Is Intact Long After Mumbai Siege," *New York Times*, September 29, 2009.

[25] K. Subrahmanyam, "War in Afghanistan," New Delhi: National Maritime Foundation, September 6, 2009, as quoted in Shanthie Mariet D'Souza, *India, Afghanistan and the 'End Game'?* Singapore: Institute of South Asian Studies, Working Paper 124, March 24, 2011, p. 18.

Report Structure

This report reviews these arguments in greater detail by comparing and contrasting India's and Pakistan's interests in Afghanistan and the ways in which each state has sought to further its objectives. The study then briefly examines how Kabul navigates the India–Pakistan rivalry to protect and advance its own interests. The paper concludes with a discussion of this competition's implications for the United States and an assessment of the Indian government's policy options for advancing its interests in Afghanistan after the U.S. military drawdown.

CHAPTER TWO

India

India's Objectives in Afghanistan

India's objectives in Afghanistan stem from a carefully calculated assessment of its domestic, regional, and global interests. Countering Pakistan's influence is certainly one of India's goals, but Delhi pursues a broad range of interests in Afghanistan that go beyond simply obstructing its principal adversary.

Prevent Anti-India Terrorism

Delhi's most fundamental goal for Afghanistan is to prevent Afghanistan from being used as a base for Pakistani-supported extremists to launch terrorist attacks in India or against Indian interests (for example, against its diplomatic missions in Afghanistan). India's Permanent Representative to the United Nations (UN) stated in July 2008 that "security within Afghanistan, and coordinated efforts to stop terrorists from operating with impunity beyond Afghanistan's borders must be the paramount priority of our collective efforts in Afghanistan."[1] Just four months later, in November 2008, assaults on multiple sites in Mumbai by Pakistani-backed Lashkar-e-Taiba (LeT) fighters hardened Indian resolve to prevent future attacks, through military means if necessary.[2]

Undermine Pakistani and Taliban Influence in Afghanistan

A related fear among some Indian thinkers is that once U.S. troops withdraw, Islamabad will move to dominate Afghanistan's political landscape, which will enable Pakistan to use the country as a safe haven and training ground for anti-Indian extremists. As the editorial page of the Indian newspaper *Mint* observed,

> Once Islamabad is assured of a friendly government in Kabul, it will unleash all the terrorists at its disposal on India. This will only mean more trouble in Jammu and Kashmir, and it will embolden terrorist groups to attack our cities with greater frequency.[3]

---

[1] Nirupam Sen, Permanent Representative from India to the United Nations, statement on the situation in Afghanistan to the United Nations Security Council, July 9, 2008, in Avtar Singh Bhasin, ed., *India's Foreign Relations, 2008: Part I*, New Delhi: Ministry of External Affairs and Geetika Publishers, 2009, p. 2534.

[2] Angel Rabasa, Robert D. Blackwill, Peter Chalk, Kim Cragin, C. Christine Fair, Brian A. Jackson, Brian Michael Jenkins, Seth G. Jones, Nathaniel Shestak, and Ashley J. Tellis, *The Lessons of Mumbai*, Santa Monica, Calif.: RAND Corporation, OP-249-RC, 2009, p. 14.

[3] "Clueless in Afghanistan," *LiveMint*, January 27, 2010.

To prevent such a development, Delhi seeks a stable, democratic, multi-ethnic Afghan government that can establish control over the whole country, maintain peace, prevent the return of the Taliban, and mitigate anti-India extremism.[4] Achieving such an arrangement, however, requires India to counter Pakistani political influence. "From the Indian perspective," writes retired Indian Brigadier Arun Sahgal, who once led the Indian military's long-range strategic planning staff,

> the most important issue is to prevent Pakistan from becoming the sole arbitrator of the Afghan political and strategic discourse, as this would not only reinforce the proxy war against India, but also fuel Islamic radicalism in the country.[5]

Increase Access to Central Asia

Both India and Pakistan need new energy sources to fuel their growing and modernizing economies. India's extraordinary economic growth of more than 7 percent annually since 1997 has made it the world's second-fastest-growing energy market, with estimates that the country will need to import more than 80 percent of its fuel by 2030.[6]

The proposed 1,000-mile, $7.6 billion Turkmenistan-Afghanistan-Pakistan-India (TAPI) pipeline would carry 33 billion cubic meters per year (bcm/y) of Turkmen gas, generating a much-needed $1.4 billion per year in transit fees for Afghanistan.[7] India and Pakistan would receive 14 bcm/y each, representing 1.5 percent of India's total annual energy consumption and 15 percent of Pakistan's.[8] The transport of Central Asian energy resources to both India and Pakistan requires stability in Afghanistan, whose territory the TAPI pipeline must cross, giving both countries strong incentives to promote security there.[9]

[4] Gautam Mukhopadhaya, "India," in Ashley J. Tellis and Aroop Mukharji, eds., *Is a Regional Strategy Viable in Afghanistan?* Washington, D.C.: Carnegie Endowment for International Peace, 2010, p. 28. See also Vishal Chandra, "The Afghan Maze and India's Options," seminar, New Delhi: Institute for Defence Studies and Analyses, September 4, 2009.

[5] Arun Sahgal, "U.S. Af-Pak Strategy and Afghanistan's Alternative Futures: Options for India," in R. K. Sawhney, Arun Sahgal, and Gurmeet Kanwal, eds., *Afghanistan: A Role for India*, New Delhi: Centre for Land Warfare Studies, 2011, p. 134.

[6] "India," *World Factbook*, Washington, D.C.: Central Intelligence Agency, updated November 8, 2011; Vibhuti Haté, "India's Energy Dilemma," *South Asia Monitor*, No. 98, September 7, 2006. With India's growing middle class seeking car ownership and consumer goods, sales of passenger and commercial vehicles grew 31 percent and 47 percent, respectively, in 2010 alone. Furthermore, 400 million people—one-third of the population—have yet to gain access to electricity. See "Indian Car Market Growth Second Fastest Globally," *Times of India*, January 12, 2011. See also U.S. Energy Information Administration, "India: Country Analysis Brief," August 2010b; and Raghav Sharma, *India and Afghanistan: Charting the Future*, New Delhi: Institute of Peace and Conflict Studies, Special Report 69, April 2009, p. 2.

[7] "Turkmenistan-Afghanistan-Pakistan-India Gas Pipeline: South Asia's Key Project," *PetroMin Pipeliner*, April–June 2011, pp. 7–8.

[8] India's share of the pipeline's capacity is equivalent to approximately one-fifth (22 percent) of India's 2010 natural gas consumption, or roughly 1.5 percent of its total energy use. Pakistan's share is more than one-third (35 percent) of its 2010 natural gas consumption, or roughly 15 percent of its total energy use (U.S. Energy Information Administration, 2010b). See also "Natural Gas Consumption Declines," *Pakistan Observer*, c. 2011; and Sajid Chaudhry, "$7.6 Billion TAPI Gas Pipeline Project," *Daily Times*, November 13, 2011.

[9] Sharma, 2009, p. 2.

Project Power and Demonstrate Global Interests

India's growth and integration into the global economy have increased the importance of commercial and trade objectives in Delhi's foreign policy. Perhaps more important is the fact that these trends have created a perception among Indians that the country is a global power and should seek to shape the world around it. "India considers its aspiration as an extra-regional power to be legitimate," Shahrbanou Tadjbakhsh of the Norwegian think tank Peace Research Institute Oslo (PRIO) has written, "commensurate with the growing size of its economy."[10]

Delhi has long used its military as a tool of projecting its influence around the world. More than 100,000 Indian troops have participated in 40 UN peacekeeping missions since the 1950s, more than 8,000 of whom are currently serving.[11] The Indian Navy has deployed ships on counterpiracy missions off the coast of Somalia, though these vessels are not formally part of the multi-national naval task force.[12] Even within the South and Central Asia regions, India's military has taken an increasingly proactive role. It built an air force base in Tajikistan, from which it transports humanitarian assistance, construction materials, and other goods into Afghanistan; the base also enables it to project military power into Central Asia.[13] India trained Kyrgyz forces in peacekeeping skills and established a framework for bilateral counter-terrorism cooperation in 2011, and, in early 2012, it resumed military cooperation with Nepal that had stalled during the latter's political turmoil.[14] India has also deployed small numbers of security forces to Afghanistan, primarily to protect Indian diplomatic missions and reconstruction projects.

Despite these moves, many Indians have a sense that their country must exert more of an influence in South Asia as a whole if it is to be taken seriously as a world power. "Afghanistan is a litmus test for [India's] ascendance as a regional and global power," writes Harsh V. Pant. "India's capacity to deal with instability in its own backyard will in the final analysis determine its rise as a global power of major import."[15] Former Indian Army Deputy Chief of Staff R. K. Sawhney writes more bluntly, "India cannot afford to beat a retreat from Afghanistan if it wants to remain a major regional player."[16]

---

[10] Tadjbakhsh, 2011, p. 33.

[11] Colum Lynch, "India Threatens to Pull Plug on Peacekeeping," *Foreign Policy*, June 14, 2011. See also "India and United Nations: Peacekeeping and Peacebuilding," United Nations, undated.

[12] The Combined Maritime Forces—often referred to by the names of its constituent Combined Task Forces (CTFs), CTF-150, CTF-151, and CTF-152—operate in the Gulf of Aden, Gulf of Oman, Arabian Sea, Red Sea, and Indian Ocean (Lauren Ploch, Christopher M. Blanchard, Ronald O'Rourke, R. Chuck Mason, and Rawle O. King, *Piracy Off the Horn of Africa*, Washington, D.C.: Congressional Research Service, R40528, April 27, 2011, p. 25). See also Combined Maritime Forces, undated web page.

[13] Pant, 2010a, p. 145.

[14] "India to Train Kyrgyz Armed Forces, Establish Military Ties in Central Asia," *Defence Now*, July 19, 2011; "India Green Lights Military Assistance to Nepal," *Himalayan*, January 18, 2012.

[15] Harsh V. Pant, "India's Changing Role: The Afghanistan Conflict," *Middle East Quarterly*, Vol. 18, No. 2, Spring 2011, pp. 31–39.

[16] R. K. Sawhney, "Afghanistan Today," in R. K. Sawhney, Arun Sahgal, and Gurmeet Kanwal, eds., *Afghanistan: A Role for India*, New Delhi: Centre for Land Warfare Studies, 2011, p. 12.

India's Strategies in Afghanistan

India is pursuing a range of strategies to advance its interests in and related to Afghanistan. In addition to seeking political and economic influence in Kabul, Delhi also strives to integrate Afghanistan into regional economic structures, offers training to Afghan security forces on a limited scale, and hopes to win Afghans' hearts and minds by providing extensive development assistance and projecting its considerable "soft power."

Seek Political Influence in Afghanistan

India has taken a range of steps to exert influence in the Afghan political sphere.

- *Support the Karzai government.* To ensure that Afghanistan does not again become a haven for Pakistani-backed terrorists, India actively seeks to garner influence in the Afghan government. It has worked to bolster the Karzai administration, build democratic institutions with multi-ethnic participation (to minimize the influence of Pashtuns), and improve the capabilities of the Afghan security forces.[17]
- *Establish a diplomatic presence.* India has also established a substantial diplomatic presence in Afghanistan to advocate for its interests. After the Taliban fell, Delhi immediately reopened its embassy in Kabul and consulates in Kandahar and Jalalabad; it later opened consulates in Herat and Mazar-e-Sharif, the major commercial centers in the western and northern parts of Afghanistan, respectively. These diplomatic posts enable India to build relationships with local leaders, facilitate trade and investment, and increase awareness of regional developments. Pakistani officials allege that Delhi also uses them to collect intelligence and support separatists in the Pakistani province of Balochistan, with the Foreign Ministry asserting that "Indian consulates in Jalalabad and Kandahar are a veritable base for RAW [Research and Analysis Wing, India's intelligence service] and its accessories."[18] Whether this is true or not, India denies the allegation.[19]
- *Keep the "northern card" in its back pocket.* During the Taliban's rule, India supported the NA, which is made up mainly of ethnic Tajiks and Uzbeks, because of its hostility to Pakistani-supported mujahideen.[20] Delhi provided the movement with weapons, materiel, equipment maintenance, and defense advisers, and the Indian military constructed a field hospital in Tajikistan for use by its fighters.[21] Some in India recommend that the government resume support to its erstwhile allies as a counterweight to Pashtun insur-

---

[17] Smruti S. Pattanaik, "India in Afghanistan: Engagement Without Strategy," *ISDA Comment*, January 28, 2011; Mukhopadhaya, 2010, p. 28.

[18] "RAW Active in Indian Consulates: Pakistan," *Dawn*, August 2, 2003.

[19] Sumit Ganguly and Nicholas Howenstein, "India–Pakistan Rivalry in Afghanistan," *Journal of International Affairs*, Vol. 63, No. 1, Fall–Winter 2009, p. 127. See also C. Christine Fair, "India in Afghanistan, Part I: Strategic Interests, Regional Concerns," *Foreign Policy*, October 26, 2010b; C. Christine Fair, "Under the Shrinking U.S. Security Umbrella: India's End Game in Afghanistan?" *Washington Quarterly*, Vol. 34, No. 2, Spring 2011a, p. 184; Arjun Verma and Teresita Schaffer, "A Difficult Road Ahead: India's Policy on Afghanistan," *South Asia Monitor*, No. 144, August 1, 2010; and Raja Karthikeya Gundu and Teresita C. Schaffer, "India and Pakistan in Afghanistan: Hostile Sports," *South Asia Monitor*, No. 117, April 3, 2008.

[20] Ganguly and Howenstein, 2009, p. 127.

[21] Fair, 2011a, p. 182.

gents and as a hedge against the Taliban's potential return.[22] Rather than serve as a deterrent to Pashtun aggression, however, such a move could end up inspiring it. Resuming military support to the NA could exacerbate tensions between Tajik-dominated northern Afghanistan and the Pashtun-dominated central administration in Kabul, leading to a much "hotter" proxy war on Afghan territory.[23] Though it is not in India's interest to stir up greater instability in Afghanistan, such an option could enable India to retaliate in kind if Pakistan increases its support to anti-Indian insurgents; if Pakistan urges its proxies to become more aggressive in India, India could urge its proxies to do the same in Afghanistan.

- *Support political reconciliation in Afghanistan.* Delhi fears that any form of reconciliation that brings the Taliban into the Afghan government will enable Pakistani-backed extremists to resume using Afghanistan as a haven in which they can safely plan and launch terror attacks against India and its interests. Addressing this concern, a prominent Indian think tank wrote, "India's security interest primarily revolves around denying any political or military space to the ISI-backed Taliban and other such fundamentalist groups."[24] India has been unsuccessful in blocking the Taliban from playing a role in Kabul, however, and it moderated its position in an effort to maintain some measure of influence. After 2010 multi-national peace talks left open the possibility of a Taliban role in government despite vociferous Indian opposition, India concluded that some form of reconciliation would happen with or without Indian support, and it accepted the idea of negotiating with insurgent leaders who renounced violence. Such a radical change in position, it seems, "represent[ed] an acknowledgement in New Delhi that it will need to have linkages with power brokers in Afghanistan whatever the composition of the government."[25] While many Indians have castigated their government for assenting to the Taliban's involvement in a future Afghan government, leaders in Delhi assessed that they would be better positioned to counter Pakistani influence if they maintain a voice in the reconciliation process than if they oppose it from outside.

Provide Development Aid and Seek Economic Influence

The Karzai government needs to improve Afghanistan's economy and create jobs to further marginalize the Taliban and improve the security situation. In a poll released by the Asia Foundation in November 2011, 45 percent of Afghans surveyed cited one of three economic issues (unemployment, poverty, or poor economy) as the greatest problem facing the country.[26] Asserting that "social and economic development is key to ensuring that Afghanistan becomes a source of regional stability,"[27] the Indian government has used a range of economic policy

---

[22] Jayanth Jacob, "India Shuffles Its Northern Card," *Hindustan Times*, August 9, 2010.

[23] Ganguly and Howenstein, 2009, p. 129.

[24] Sharma, 2009, p. 2.

[25] Verma and Schaffer, 2010.

[26] Mohammed Osman Tariq, Najla Ayoubi, and Fazel Rabi Haqbeen, *Afghanistan in 2011: A Survey of the Afghan People*, Kabul: Asia Foundation, 2011, pp. 23–26.

[27] External Publicity Division, Ministry of External Affairs, Government of India, *India and Afghanistan: A Development Partnership*, c. 2009, p. 8.

tools—including development assistance, trade promotion, and private investment—to promote stability and increase Indian influence in the country:

- *Development assistance:* India provides more foreign aid to Afghanistan than to any other country.[28] It is Afghanistan's fifth-most significant source of development assistance and its largest South Asian donor.[29] As of early 2011, Delhi had provided $1.3 billion in aid to Afghanistan, though subsequent pledges have raised the total amount committed since 2001 to $2 billion.[30] Indian initiatives have promoted the legitimacy of the Karzai administration, both by offering programs to enhance good governance and by focusing Indian support on President Karzai's development priorities—infrastructure, education, training, health care, agriculture, telecommunications, power generation, and civil aviation.[31] Projects range from small, community-level projects to the construction of large-scale power generation and transmission infrastructure.[32] Despite India's intent to continue providing development assistance to Kabul, the poor security environment in Afghanistan has clearly affected Delhi's willingness to start new projects. Indeed, as of June 2011, India had not launched any major initiatives for the previous two to three years.[33] Although Delhi deployed 500 members of the Indo-Tibetan Border Police (ITBP) to secure Indian development workers and diplomatic facilities after a series of high-profile attacks,[34] the continuing unstable security situation in Afghanistan may require Indian policymakers to consider augmenting this presence with additional troops.
- *Trade:* In 2003, Delhi and Kabul signed a preferential trade agreement that reduced duties on Afghan exports, primarily agricultural goods.[35] This was an extremely important accord given that fully one-quarter of Afghanistan's exports are destined for Indian

---

[28] "India's Role in Afghanistan," *IISS Strategic Comments*, Vol. 17, June 2011.

[29] Fair, 2011a, p. 180. See also Shiza Shahid, *Engaging Regional Players in Afghanistan*, Washington, D.C.: Center for Strategic and International Studies, November 24, 2009, p. 2. Rankings of donors vary, depending on whether the analyst focuses on amounts pledged, amounts dispersed, percentage of pledges disbursed, and other factors. In November 2009, Afghanistan's Ministry of Finance ranked India as its seventh-largest donor in terms of aid commitments, with a total of $1.236 billion pledged, following the United States, United Kingdom, European Union (EU) and European Commission (EC), World Bank, the Asian Development Bank, and Japan. See Ministry of Finance, Islamic Republic of Afghanistan, *Donor Financial Review*, Report 1388, November 2009, p. 40.

[30] The $1.3 billion figure is taken from Robert O. Blake Jr., assistant secretary, Bureau of South and Central Asian Affairs, U.S. Department of State, "The Obama Administration's Priorities in South and Central Asia," remarks, Houston, Texas, January 19, 2011a. See also "Obama Appreciates India's Role in Afghanistan," *The Hindu*, November 7, 2010; and "India's Role in Afghanistan," 2011.

[31] See Pratibha Devisingh Patil, president of India, speech at the banquet in honor of the president of the Islamic Republic of Afghanistan, Hamid Karzai, New Delhi, August 4, 2008, in Bhasin, 2009, p. 1201.

[32] External Publicity Division, 2009, pp. 19–20, 26–31.

[33] "India's Role in Afghanistan," 2011.

[34] Jayshree Bajoria, "India-Afghanistan Relations," Council on Foreign Relations backgrounder, July 22, 2009. See also Shanthie Mariet D'Souza, "Hold Steady in Afghanistan," *Pragati: The Indian National Interest Review*, No. 17, August 2008, pp. 9–11. The ITBP were deployed in a purely protective role and were given no mandate to work at the sites of private Indian companies.

[35] "Indo-Afghan Commercial Relations," Embassy of India in Kabul, undated.

markets, with bilateral trade expected to reach as much as $1 billion by 2012.[36] At present, Delhi must send commodities to Afghanistan via Iran because Pakistan prevents Indian goods from crossing its territory. Should Islamabad remove this restriction, Indian–Afghan trade will expand dramatically.

- *Private investment:* Indian companies are entering the Afghan market in droves, particularly in the agriculture, manufacturing, telecommunications, and mining sectors. Notably, in late 2011, no fewer than 14 Indian firms bid on an iron mining contract in Bamyan province that could generate $6 billion in investment.[37] President Karzai asked Indian Prime Minister Manmohan Singh to encourage yet more Indian investment at the November 2011 South Asian Association for Regional Cooperation (SAARC) summit in the Maldives, and Afghan Commerce and Industries Minister Anwar-Ul-Haq Ahady made a similar pitch to Indian small and medium enterprises in Delhi the previous month.[38] These overtures bode well for future expansions of bilateral investment links in the coming years.

Although India's reconstruction strategy is designed to highlight Indian munificence, expand trade, and gain political advantage in Afghanistan, it is also clearly intended to undercut Pakistani influence there.[39] By constructing a 220-kilometer road between the Afghan cities of Zaranj and Delaram in 2008–2009, for example, the Indian Border Roads Organization (BRO) connected the main Herat-Kandahar highway with existing routes leading to the Iranian port of Chabahar. (See Figure 2.1.) It is no coincidence, however, that the road will significantly shorten overland journey times to a commercial ocean outlet and will be much faster than the present network that connects Afghanistan to the Pakistani ports of Karachi and Gwadar.[40] Similarly, to facilitate Indian companies' access to Afghanistan's estimated $1 trillion in minerals and raw materials, Delhi is planning to build a rail link from Hajigak, a mineral-rich area in Bamyan province, through Zaranj, and onward to Chabahar (see Figure 2.2).[41] India is also working with Iran to build a 600-km road from Chabahar to the Iranian city of Zahedan, near the southwestern corner of Afghanistan, that would follow a similar route to the rail line.[42] Although these transit routes will reduce the amount of time it takes for Afghan goods to reach a major port, the primary benefit will accrue to India. Not only will the new route facilitate Indian–Afghan trade; it will also prevent Islamabad from

---

[36] Geoffrey Pyatt, principal deputy assistant secretary, Bureau of South and Central Asian Affairs, U.S. Department of State, "Next Steps on the Silk Road," remarks to members of the Federation of Indian Chambers of Commerce and Industry, Chennai, November 15, 2011.

[37] Simbal Khan, "India's Planned Investment in Afghanistan," *Express Tribune*, September 9, 2011. See also Sanjeev Miglani, "Indian Firms Eye Huge Mining Investment in Afghanistan," Reuters, September 14, 2011.

[38] "Afghanistan Wants Indian Investments: Singh," *Daily Outlook Afghanistan*, November 14, 2011.

[39] "India: Afghanistan's Influential Ally," BBC News, October 8, 2009. See also Sharma, 2009, p. 3; and D'Souza, 2011, pp. 9–10.

[40] Sudha Ramachandran, "India Takes a Slow Road," *Asia Times*, January 27, 2007.

[41] Jayanth Jacob and Saubhadra Chatterji, "India's Track 3: Afghan–Iran Rail Link," *Hindustan Times*, November 1, 2011.

[42] Jyoti Malhotra, "Iran's Chabahar Port Eclipses Pakistan in Race for Afghan Profits," *Business Standard*, July 2, 2012.

Figure 2.1
Afghan Road Connections to Iran and Turkmenistan

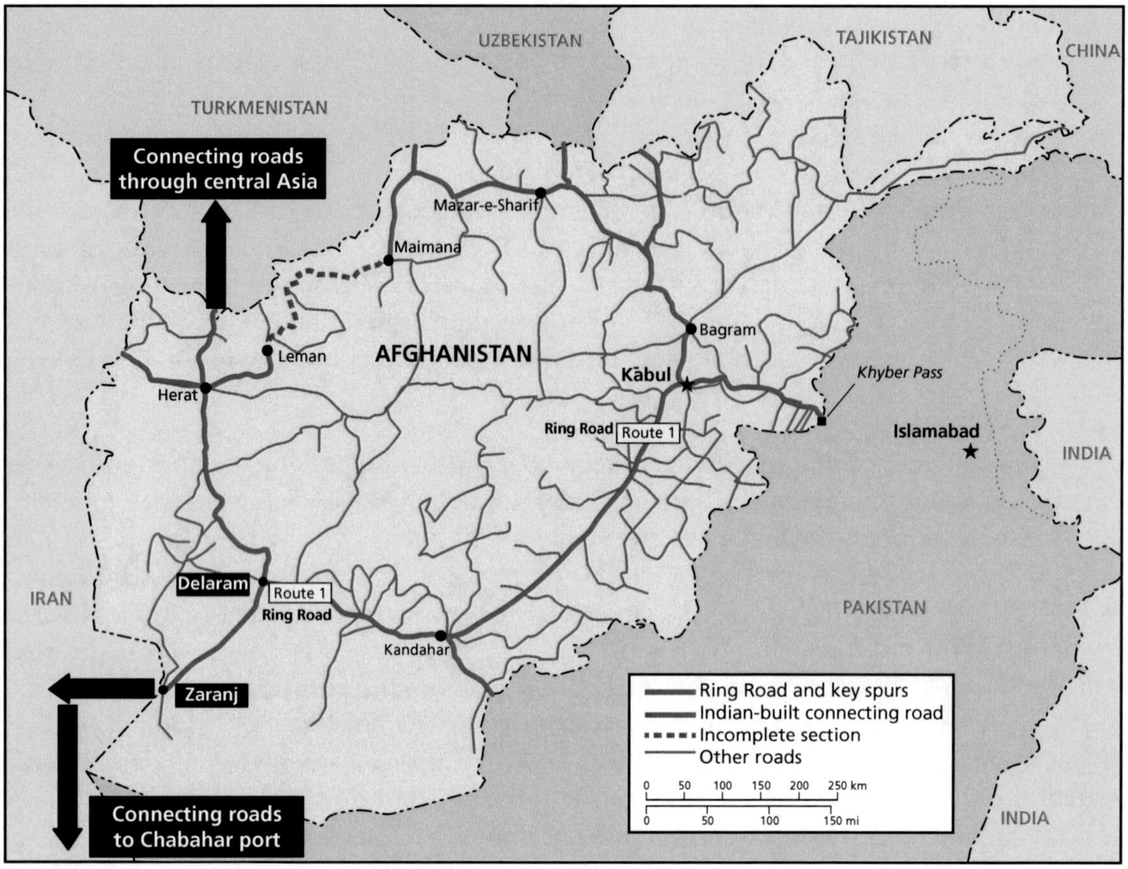

SOURCES: Asian Development Bank; Stratfor, "Afghanistan Battle Ring Road," March 16, 2010, used with permission.
RAND OP387-2.1

continuing to block Indian exports to Afghanistan and undermine the importance of Pakistan's Gwadar port, which was built at considerable cost with significant Chinese investment.[43]

The enormous security challenges associated with these road and rail infrastructure projects highlights that they are intended to advance India's strategic interest in gaining access to Afghan minerals and markets rather than simply to generate commercial activity. Both the Zaranj–Delaram road and the planned Bamyan–Chabahar railroad pass through Taliban-dominated Nimroz province, thus enabling the Taliban (and, presumably, its Pakistani backers) to disrupt Indian commerce along these routes.[44] For these transit links to be truly effective, therefore, security in this region would have to be significantly improved—perhaps by Indian security forces, if Delhi were to decide to deploy them to protect Indian development

---

[43] Interestingly, by October 2011, the Indian-built road was reported to be under Taliban control. It is unclear whether the Taliban simply took advantage of U.S. troop redeployments, sought to make use of a strategic corridor, or, as one Indian newspaper suggested, take the road at Pakistan's direction in order to block Indian trade. See V. K. Shashikumar, "Indian Built Zaranj–Delaram Highway Under Taliban Control," *Indian Defence Review*, October 1, 2011.

[44] Shashikumar, 2011. See also Dean Nelson, "India Plans 'World's Most Dangerous Railroad' from Afghanistan to Iran," *Telegraph*, November 2, 2011.

Figure 2.2
Bamyan–Chabahar Railroad

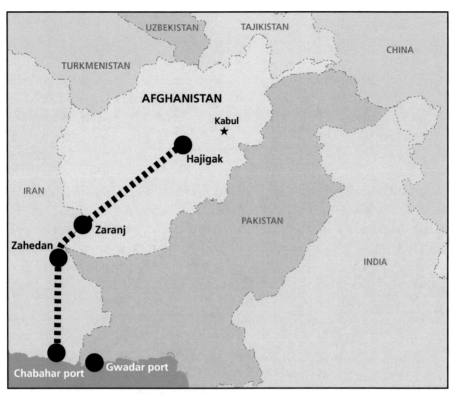

SOURCES: Jacob and Chatterji, 2011; Malhotra, 2012.
RAND *OP387-2.2*

projects—or the Taliban would have to be given an incentive to permit commerce to pass unmolested.

Regionalize Solutions to Afghan Security and Stability Problems

India has pursued regional solutions to Afghanistan's security and stability problems to give governments throughout South and Central Asia stakes in its success and, in the words of India's external affairs minister, to enable all countries in the region to "advance together through free trade, open borders, and regional economic integration.[45] This multi-lateral approach also has the added benefit of diluting Islamabad's influence over Afghan affairs, which, in turn, as an Indian think-tank researcher writes, helps "enable Kabul to be more independent and less subject to Pakistani arm twisting."[46]

An important strand of Delhi's regional approach has been to promote Afghanistan's membership in SAARC, both to institutionalize the country's integration with its neighbors

---

[45] Ashley J. Tellis, "Implementing a Regional Approach to Afghanistan: Multiple Alternatives, Modest Possibilities," in Ashley J. Tellis and Aroop Mukharji, eds., *Is a Regional Strategy Viable in Afghanistan?* Washington, D.C.: Carnegie Endowment for International Peace, 2010, p. 97; quote from Pranab Mukherjee, external affairs minister, "India and the Global Balance of Power," address on the occasion of the national launch of the Global India Foundation, January 16, 2007a, in Avtar Singh Bhasin, ed., *India's Foreign Relations, 2007: Part I*, New Delhi: Ministry of External Affairs and Geetika Publishers, 2008, p. 139.

[46] Mukhopadhaya, 2010, p. 28; quote from Pattanaik, 2011.

and to foster greater two-way trade between these states.[47] Integrating Afghanistan into the regional economy could generate as much as $2 billion in regional activity, including $600 million for Afghanistan.[48] Such a strategy also helps establish Afghanistan as a viable land bridge between India and the energy-rich CARs.[49]

Although much of their interaction has been zero-sum in nature, Delhi and Islamabad did manage to agree on one critical regional project that would yield mutual benefits: the 1,000-mile TAPI gas pipeline that would provide sorely needed natural gas to both India and Pakistan.[50] As discussed, both countries' growing energy requirements give their governments a vested interest in ensuring a stable Afghanistan, through whose territory the pipeline must transit.[51]

Project Power

Whether to deploy additional security forces to protect its aid and investment projects has become a significant debate for India as it reconsiders its Afghanistan policy. However, this question is just one element of a broader discussion about how India can project power in South Asia and beyond. "The dilemma confronting Indian policy-makers on Afghanistan is not merely limited to the country's specific interests and engagement in the reconstruction activities," writes Indian academic Shantie Mariet D'Souza, "but stems from India's quest to play a larger role in regional and global affairs."[52]

Indian military strategy has increasingly called for more expeditionary forces that can project power throughout South Asia and the Indian Ocean region by, for example, protecting sea lines of communication used for maritime trade and energy shipments. It has also acquired assets useful for out-of-area operations, such as aircraft carriers and long-range bombers capable of midair refueling, and military leaders have expressed desires for aircraft forward-basing arrangements and increased access to ports throughout the Indian Ocean. That said, India's operational capabilities remain limited, and its recent overseas deployments have primarily been for humanitarian purposes, such as the evacuation of South Asian civilians from Lebanon in 2006 and the delivery of relief supplies to tsunami-stricken Indonesia, Sri Lanka, and Maldives in 2004.[53]

By playing a critical role in Afghanistan's security and economic development, India hopes to shape regional developments and project power throughout South Asia and beyond. Indian Foreign Secretary Nirupama Rao asserted that India's emergence as a world power requires

---

[47] Pranab Mukherjee, external affairs minister, speech at the Research and Information System for Developing Countries and South Asia Centre for Policy Studies Conference, "Economic Cooperation in SAARC: SAFTA and Beyond," New Delhi, March 19, 2007b, in Bhasin, 2008, p. 1016.

[48] Pant, 2011, p. 33.

[49] Using Afghanistan as such a land bridge, of course, requires the cooperation of either Pakistan or Iran (Mukhopadhaya, 2010, p. 32).

[50] Atul Aneja, "India and Afghanistan: The Way Forward," The Hindu, January 4, 2011.

[51] Marvin G. Weinbaum and Haseeb Humayoon, "The Intertwined Destinies of Afghanistan and Pakistan," in J. Alexander Thier, ed., The Future of Afghanistan, Washington, D.C.: U.S. Institute of Peace, 2009, p. 98.

[52] D'Souza, 2008, p. 9.

[53] Walter C. Ladwig III, "India and Military Power Projection: Will the Land of Gandhi Become a Conventional Great Power?" Asian Survey, Vol. 50, No. 6, November–December 2010, pp. 1171–1174, 1177–1179. Also Peter R. Lavoy, "India in 2006: A New Emphasis on Engagement," Asian Survey, Vol. 47, No. 1, January–February 2007, pp. 119, 121–122.

"a peaceful and stable neighborhood and external environment," which suggests that India sees stability in Afghanistan as a key prerequisite to achieving its overarching strategic goals.[54] Kings College London professor Harsh V. Pant asserts that "the success of India's Afghanistan policy will go a long way in determining if India will be able to emerge as a provider of regional security in South Asia."[55] Furthermore, by reaching through Afghanistan into the CARs, Delhi has the potential to shape events there, both as a consumer of Central Asian oil and gas and as a counterweight to Chinese and Russian influence. Thus, although C. Christine Fair writes that India's activities in Afghanistan are "about India's emergent ability to influence its extended strategic neighborhood,"[56] they also earn Delhi a measure of respect on the international stage by enabling the country "to be, and *to be seen*, as an extra-regional power moving toward great power status."[57]

India is also able to project a considerable amount of soft power. As a multi-ethnic, democratic society with a thriving economy and vibrant media, the country projects a very positive image. Its Bollywood movie industry—which makes upward of 800 wildly popular films every year—portrays glamorous lifestyles and extravagant events.[58] These cultural products have extensively penetrated the Afghan market; indeed, one of the most widely watched television shows in Afghanistan for a time was an Indian soap opera dubbed into Dari.[59]

Grassroots-level Indian aid projects have also helped to project a favorable image of India among ordinary Afghans. Many of its aid programs are deliberately high-profile, such as the construction of a new parliament building, the donation of planes to Ariana Afghan Airlines, and the construction of a large pediatric hospital in Kabul named after Indira Gandhi.[60] In addition to education and training programs and the construction of vocational schools and clinics, Delhi has delivered humanitarian assistance and offered free medical care for more than 350,000 Afghans in a period of less than two years.[61] These and other reconstruction initiatives have provided India with a ready-made conduit through which to win Afghans' hearts and minds.[62] In part for this purpose, Delhi has spread its development aid across Afghanistan to ensure that all regional and ethnic groups in that country have benefited from Indian largesse.[63]

[54] Nirupama Rao, foreign secretary, speech at the French Institute of International Relations, Paris, May 5, 2011.

[55] Harsh V. Pant, *India's Challenge in Afghanistan: With Power Comes Responsibility*, Philadelphia, Pa.: Center for the Advanced Study of India, Working Paper 10-02, March 2010b, p. 2.

[56] Fair, 2010b.

[57] C. Christine Fair, *India in Afghanistan and Beyond: Opportunities and Constraints*, Washington, D.C.: Century Foundation, 2010a, p. 4. Emphasis in the original.

[58] "What Is Bollywood?" *Newsround*, undated. Of course, many conservative Afghans view Bollywood films' romantic plot lines and lascivious dance routines less positively.

[59] Shashi Tharoor, "Hooray for Bollywood: India's 'Soft Power,'" *Taipei Times*, January 7, 2008.

[60] Emily Wax, "India's Eager Courtship of Afghanistan Comes at a Steep Price," *Washington Post*, April 3, 2010; External Publicity Division, 2009, pp. 14, 22.

[61] "India's Role in Afghanistan," 2011. See also External Publicity Division, 2009, p. 9.

[62] Gundu and Schaffer, 2008.

[63] "India's Role in Afghanistan," 2011. See also Indian Ambassador to Afghanistan Jayant Prasad, quoted in "We Have Only Four Consulates in Afghanistan, Exactly the Same Number We Had Earlier," *Rediff News*, February 26, 2009.

Finally, Delhi has made a conscious effort to cultivate ties with Afghan elites who have long-standing ties to India or to movements backed by it.[64] President Karzai, for example, attended university in Himachal Pradesh during the Soviet occupation,[65] while former foreign minister and presidential candidate Abdullah Abdullah, former parliament speaker Younus Qanooni, and other senior officials played important roles in the Indian-supported NA while the Taliban was in power.[66]

Provide Military Assistance

The one area in which India has not projected its power into Afghanistan is through military might. Though Delhi deployed some 500 ITBP personnel to protect Indian aid workers and diplomats on their compounds, these troops were not tasked with any offensive counter-insurgency (COIN) or stabilization missions. Further, although Delhi has provided limited training to the Afghan National Army in India,[67] it has eschewed greater military involvement for a range of reasons. Most notably, Indian leaders realize that India's troops would make easy targets for Afghan militants and that an Indian military deployment to Afghanistan could embolden anti-India extremists in Kashmir, which has been increasingly peaceful in recent years.

In recent months, however, India seems to have taken a more assertive approach regarding military cooperation with Afghanistan. As part of a strategic partnership agreement signed by Afghan President Hamid Karzai and Indian Prime Minister Manmohan Singh in October 2011, Delhi agreed to provide light weapons, as well as training in COIN and high-altitude warfare, to the Afghan army, police, and air force.[68] The accord stops far short of calling for the dispatch of Indian troops to Afghanistan. Nevertheless, by committing to provide military instruction, Delhi has decided to engage in a bilateral security partnership with Kabul despite Pakistani opposition.

Effectiveness of India's Strategies

Delhi's success in projecting political, economic, commercial, and cultural influence has furthered its desire to be seen as a contributor to regional security, and India has been very effective at advancing its strategic interests in Afghanistan. The Karzai government has responded positively to Indian initiatives by strengthening its political, economic, and diplomatic ties with Delhi despite Pakistan's clear displeasure.[69] Indian support for Kabul's membership in

---

[64] Ishaan Tharoor, "India, Pakistan and the Battle for Afghanistan," *Time*, December 5, 2009.

[65] "Biography," Office of the President, Islamic Republic of Afghanistan, undated.

[66] I. Tharoor, 2009.

[67] India has trained 200 Afghan Army officers and 50 military cadets at Indian military academies to date, and it has offered to train up to 100 Afghan cadets annually in the future. See Shashank Joshi, "India's Strategic Calculus in Afghanistan," *Foreign Policy*, October 6, 2011. See also Manu Pubby, "50 Afghan Cadets Train at IMA," *Indian Express*, July 22, 2011.

[68] "India Decides to Train Afghanistan's Army and Signs Other Bilateral Agreements with Afghanistan," *Defence Now*, October 7, 2011. See also Sumit Ganguly, "India and the Afghan Endgame," *Diplomat*, November 14, 2011; and "Indo-Afghan Strategic Partnership," *Daily Times*, October 6, 2011.

[69] Robert D. Kaplan, "Behind the Indian Embassy Bombing," *Atlantic*, August 2008.

SAARC and its construction of road and rail links will integrate Afghanistan into the South and Central Asian regions and provide India with access to important trade routes and energy markets in Central Asia.

In addition to winning the support of the Karzai government, Delhi has also earned the respect of ordinary Afghans. The extent of popular support for India—a by-product of its "no-strings-attached"[70] strategy of reconstruction assistance, soft power projection, and outreach to all major Afghan ethnic groups[71]—is particularly striking when compared with Afghans' perceptions of Pakistan. A 2009 ABC News/BBC poll, for example, found that "74 percent of Afghans held favorable opinions of India, while 8 percent hold favorable opinions toward Pakistan."[72] Delhi's non-participation in military activities taking place in Afghanistan has likely helped cultivate India's image as a positive contributor to Afghanistan rather than as an outside meddler.[73] This stands in stark contrast to Pakistan, which 86 percent of Afghans believe plays a negative role in Afghanistan.[74]

However, the return of the Taliban in any significant way could wreck most of what Delhi has accomplished to date and derail future initiatives. Such a development would enable Afghan territory to be used once again as a launching pad for militant attacks on India, place Kabul back in the Pakistani orbit, and effectively put an end to Indian aid, investment, and trade in Afghanistan. In accepting that some form of political reconciliation process is inevitable—and that continued Indian objections to it would have little effect—India may have gained some ability to block the inclusion of strongly pro-Pakistan figures in a future Kabul government, which, if successful, could mitigate these developments.

---

[70] Satish Chandra, "India's Options in Afghanistan," *Strategic Analysis*, Vol. 35, No. 1, January 2011, p. 125.

[71] Ashley J. Tellis, "Creating New Facts on the Ground: Why the Diplomatic Surge Cannot Yet Produce a Regional Solution in Afghanistan," Washington, D.C.: Carnegie Endowment for International Peace, Policy Brief 91, May 2011, p. 5.

[72] "Support for U.S. Efforts Plummets Amid Afghanistan's Ongoing Strife," ABC News/BBC/ARD poll, February 9, 2009, p. 12.

[73] D'Souza, 2008, p. 9.

[74] Ganguly and Howenstein, 2009, p. 136. Also see "Support for U.S. Efforts Plummets Amid Afghanistan's Ongoing Strife," 2009, p. 12.

CHAPTER THREE
Pakistan

Pakistan's Objectives in Afghanistan

Pakistan's goals in Afghanistan are mainly India-centric and focus primarily on undermining Delhi's influence in Afghanistan while promoting its own. Islamabad thus seeks to maximize Taliban influence in a weak Kabul government, maintain "strategic depth" against an Indian invasion, and facilitate training and operations by Pakistani-backed extremist groups. However, these are not Pakistan's only concerns. Other important priorities include marginalizing historical Afghan claims on Pakistani territory and (just as India desires) developing trade with the CARs.

Block Indian Influence

Pakistan has long considered India to be an aggressive state that poses a fundamental threat to its territorial integrity. Not only does Islamabad blame Delhi for orchestrating the creation of Bangladesh out of East Pakistan in 1971, but it is acutely aware of India's demographic, geographic, economic, and military advantages.[1] Its military leadership has a zero-sum view of the Indian-Pakistani dynamic, seeing anything that benefits India as a loss for Pakistan. Thus, according to Frédéric Grare, a former French diplomat with expertise in South Asia, "According to Pakistan, whatever India does in Afghanistan is a ploy against Pakistan, be it economic investment, infrastructure, or any related matter. . . . As a result, Pakistan has ensured that Indian interests would be blocked whenever and wherever possible."[2]

Prevent Encirclement and Maintain Strategic Depth

Unable to believe that Indian leaders might pursue interests for reasons other than gaining advantage against Pakistan, Islamabad perceives India's efforts to gain influence in Afghanistan as a deliberate strategy of encirclement that is aimed at trapping and ultimately destroying

---

[1] Pakistan's defense budget is one-quarter that of India's, and its gross domestic product (GDP) is only $175 billion, compared with India's $1.4 trillion. India's population is roughly ten times the size of Pakistan's, providing India with a far larger pool of military manpower on which to draw. Finally, whereas India is approximately one-third the size of the United States, Pakistan is less than twice the size of California. See David M. Abshire and Ryan Browne, "The Missing Endgame for Afghanistan: A Sustainable Post–bin Laden Strategy," *Washington Quarterly*, Vol. 34, No. 4, Fall 2011, p. 69. See also "India," 2011, and "Pakistan," *World Factbook*, Washington, D.C.: Central Intelligence Agency, last updated June 7, 2012.

[2] Frédéric Grare, "Pakistan," in Ashley J. Tellis and Aroop Mukharji, eds., *Is a Regional Strategy Viable in Afghanistan?* Washington, D.C.: Carnegie Endowment for International Peace, 2010, p. 21.

Pakistan between hostile fronts.[3] Islamabad's overriding objective in Afghanistan is therefore to block Delhi's own penetration into the country by helping to foster a pro-Pakistani administration in Kabul.[4]

Although Islamabad thus sees a friendly regime in Kabul as necessary to keep India out, the army also maintains that a weak, subservient government in Afghanistan is needed to ensure that Pakistan has sufficient strategic depth—the ability to retreat to Afghan territory, if necessary, to repel an Indian invasion.[5] Although this concept has long been, and still remains, a hallowed doctrine within the Pakistani military, some analysts believe that it is somewhat outdated in the nuclear era because the mere threat of nuclear retaliation makes an overwhelming Indian invasion unlikely in the first place.[6]

Establish Safe Havens for Pakistani-Trained Extremists

A pro-Pakistani Afghan state would furnish Islamabad with a rear base in which to train Islamist militants—such as Harakat-ul-Mujahideen (HuM) and Jaish-e-Mohammed (JeM), in addition to LeT—for non-attributable attacks in Jammu, Kashmir, and elsewhere in India. The use of jihadist proxies is an established tenet of Pakistan's foreign policy and one of the principal means by which the ISI has prosecuted the government's national security strategy vis-à-vis Delhi.[7] Ensuring a continued safe haven outside Pakistani territory would allow Islamabad to sustain its so-called war of a thousand cuts while enabling it to deny direct sponsorship of terrorism.

Pakistan's control over these surrogate groups allows it to calibrate the level of extremist violence against India, a capability that acts as an important defense against Indian aggression and a tool that can both deter Indian outreach to Afghanistan and undermine Indian successes there after the fact. Thus, although a more assertive Indian presence in Afghanistan could

---

[3]   Because Islamabad views Afghanistan through the prism of its hostile relations with Delhi, any Indian push into the western neighbor can only be interpreted in zero-sum terms and as a deliberately orchestrated, malicious action designed to exploit extant indigenous tensions in Afghanistan. See, for instance, Ganguly and Howenstein, 2009, pp. 134–135. See also William Maley, "Afghanistan and Its Region," in J. Alexander Thier, ed., *The Future of Afghanistan*, Washington, D.C.: U.S. Institute of Peace, 2009, p. 84; Abshire and Browne, 2011, p. 69; and Elizabeth Roche, "India, Pakistan's 'Proxy War' in Afghanistan," Agence France-Presse, March 3, 2010.

[4]   Ben Arnoldy, "How the Afghanistan War Became Tangled in India vs. Pakistan Rivalry," *Christian Science Monitor*, January 20, 2011.

[5]   Strategic depth is a doctrinal concept of the Pakistani military and is based on the idea that, if Pakistan's forces were overpowered by an Indian invasion, they could fall back to Afghan territory and continue to fight from there. See Ahmed Rashid, *Taliban: Islam, Oil and the New Great Game in Central Asia*, London: I. B. Tauris, 2000, pp. 186–187. See also Marvin G. Weinbaum and Jonathan B. Harder, "Pakistan's Afghan Policies and Their Consequences," *Contemporary South Asia*, Vol. 16, No. 1, 2008, p. 26; and Sushant K. Singh, "A Bigger Military Presence Is Essential If India Is to Shape Afghanistan's Future," *Pragati: The Indian National Interest Review*, No. 17, August 2008, p. 12.

[6]   Indian Ambassador to Afghanistan Jayant Prasad, quoted in "We Have Only Four Consulates in Afghanistan," 2009. See also Sawhney, 2011, p. 10.

[7]   See, for instance, Fair and Chalk, 2006, pp. 68–69. See also Imtiaz Gul, "Pakistan's New Networks of Terror," *Foreign Policy*, June 10, 2010, p. 2; Sundeep Waslekar, Leena Pillai, and Shabnam Siddiqui, *The Future of Pakistan*, Mumbai: Strategic Foresight Group, 2002, pp. 51–59; and Jessica Stern, "Pakistan's Jihad Culture," *Foreign Affairs*, November–December 2000.

prevent terror attacks in India by eliminating extremists' Afghan safe havens, Indian policies could also inspire Pakistan to ramp up anti-Indian violence in response.[8]

Undermine Afghan Claims on Pashtunistan

Islamabad also seeks to fend off Afghan claims on Pakistani territory, which have been a consistent thorn in bilateral relations given that no Afghan regime has ever accepted the legitimacy of the border drawn by the British in 1893, the so-called Durand Line.[9] Pakistan thus seeks to foster a compliant regime in Kabul that dampens Pashtun nationalism and concomitant calls for an independent Pashtun homeland in parts of Balochistan, the FATA, and KPK. Calls for a breakaway irredentist Pashtunistan would directly threaten Pakistan's territorial integrity and potentially contribute to its disintegration along ethnic lines.[10]

As Ahmed Rashid notes, Pakistan wrongly calculated that its extensive political and military assistance would lead the Taliban to recognize the Durand Line, curb Pashtun nationalism in KPK, and serve as an outlet for Pakistan's disgruntled Islamic radicals who might otherwise direct their ire at the Pakistani state. In fact, the opposite occurred. The Taliban refused to recognize the Durand Line or drop Afghanistan's claims to parts of KPK. The Taliban fostered Pashtun nationalism, imbuing it with a greater religious character, in a manner that appealed to Pakistani Pashtuns.[11]

Build Economic Links to the Central Asian Republics

Pakistan would like to use Afghanistan as a conduit for enhancing regional commerce and transportation links with the CARs, just as India seeks to do. A strong Pakistani grip on northern trade routes would diminish the value of Iran's Chabahar port and the Indian-built Zaranj–Delaram road (which connects to the Kushka-Herat-Kandahar highway), thereby undermining India's efforts to expand its own economic ties with Afghanistan and Central Asia.[12]

Furthermore, Pakistan is eager to gain access to Central Asian natural gas. Rapid economic growth has caused demand for energy to rise far more quickly than domestic production; energy shortages, which lead to frequent blackouts, are severe. Pakistan's federal minister for petroleum and natural resources, Asim Hussain, warned in January 2012 that, unless Pakistan identifies new sources of natural gas quickly, "the whole energy system of the country

---

[8] In March 2010, Pakistan Army chief of staff Ashfaq Parvez Kayani and ISI director Ahmad Shuja Pasha told President Karzai that Pakistan could "cool down" the Taliban insurgency but that Afghanistan would have to eliminate India's presence in Afghanistan in exchange. See Steve Coll, "War by Other Means," *New Yorker*, May 24, 2010, p. 51.

[9] The Durand Line was drawn in 1893 and split ethnic Pashtuns between Afghanistan and British colonial India. No Afghan regime has ever accepted the international boundary as legitimate. See Rashid, 2000, p. 187. See also Fair and Chalk, 2006, p. 75.

[10] Weinbaum and Humayoon, 2009, p. 96. See also Weinbaum and Harder, 2008, p. 26; and Tellis, 2011, p. 1.

[11] Rashid, 2010, p. 187.

[12] Mukhopadhaya, 2010, p. 34. See also Rashid, 2000, p. 90; Meena Singh Roy, "Pakistan's Strategies in Central Asia," *Strategic Analysis*, Vol. 30, No. 4, October–December 2006, p. 802; and Ganguly and Howenstein, 2009, p. 136.

could collapse."[13] By 2016, Pakistan is expected to import 48 percent of its natural gas (which makes up nearly half of its energy consumption).[14]

Curb Other States' Influence in Afghanistan

In addition to limiting Indian power projection in Afghanistan, Pakistan seeks to limit the extent to which other states are able to extend their influence in Afghanistan. This is particularly true of Iran, Russia, and the United States. Islamabad's relationship with Tehran has always been uneasy, reflecting the latter's alleged support of Shi'a militias operating in Balochistan and lingering suspicions of Iranian involvement in the mysterious death of former Pakistani President Muhammad Zia ul-Haq. Moreover, Iran has managed to garner a relatively high degree of support among the Afghan Shi'a communities along the border with Pakistani Balochistan—an area in which Pakistan has traditionally enjoyed very little influence. From Islamabad's perspective, any further expansion of Iranian influence in this area could foster instability in the historically restive Balochistan province.

Pakistan views creeping Russian involvement in Afghanistan with equal ambivalence. Not surprisingly, the Soviet occupation of Afghanistan in the 1980s has left senior officers in the army and ISI—many of whom started their careers as trainers for the anti-Soviet mujahideen—highly suspicious of Russia's interests and motives in Afghanistan. Islamabad is thus wary of Moscow's historical ties with India and the former Soviet CARs and its past role in supporting the Uzbek-, Tajik-, and Hazara-dominated NA.[15]

To some degree, Pakistan lumps the United States in with other countries that seek to exercise influence in Afghanistan to Pakistan's detriment because some Pakistani politicians view U.S. involvement in Afghanistan more as a threat than as a comfort. Washington's diplomatic efforts to broker a peace deal between the Taliban and Kabul have added to this consternation by engendering fears that Washington will drive a settlement that does not take into account or, worse, actively bypasses Islamabad's own interests and perceived prerogatives.[16]

Pakistan's Strategies in Afghanistan

Train Extremists to Counter India in Afghanistan

In pursuing its primary objectives in Afghanistan, Pakistan has relied on a variety of strategies. Most directly, it has backed proxies to attack Indian interests in Afghanistan. The ISI is widely believed to have provided extensive assistance to the Taliban and Haqqani network in the form of training, funding, munitions, supplies, and safe haven (notably in Karachi and the tribal areas of Balochistan), and it is thought to retain considerable influence over both movements.[17]

---

[13] "Asim Hussain Paints a Dire Picture of the Gas Crisis," *Express Tribune*, January 3, 2012.

[14] "Pakistan Consumes Half of Its Gas Reserves," *Daily Times*, December 28, 2011. See also "Pakistan Oil and Gas Report Q4 2011," *Business Monitor International*, September 16, 2011.

[15] Rashid, 2010, p. 5.

[16] See, for instance, "U.S. Set to Ignore Pakistan, Afghanistan in Taliban Talks," *Press TV*, February 10, 2012.

[17] Admiral Mike Mullen, chairman of the Joint Chiefs of Staff, told a congressional committee in September 2011 that the Haqqani network "acts as a veritable arm of Pakistan's intelligence." Furthermore, the Quetta Shura Taliban (QST), the umbrella organization that provides direction and guidance for the campaign to create a so-called Islamic Emirate of Afghanistan (IEA) and that includes both the Taliban and Haqqani network, is widely believed to operate directly from

In the assessment of the U.S. Director of National Intelligence (DNI), this support is a critical element in Pakistan's strategic arsenal to counter Delhi's military, political, and economic presence in Afghanistan.[18] Both groups—which are engaged primarily in fighting U.S.-led coalition forces—are believed to have conducted strikes aimed specifically at India, likely with Pakistani support.[19] Three examples stand out: the July 7, 2008, suicide bombing of Delhi's embassy in Kabul, which killed 58 and wounded 141; a second attack on the embassy on October 8, 2009, which left 17 people dead and 63 wounded; and the February 26, 2010, leveling of the Hamid Guesthouse, a hotel in the heart of the capital that was popular with Indian doctors and reconstruction workers, which resulted in 18 fatalities and an additional 36 casualties.[20]

Several commentators have also alleged that Islamabad has deliberately redirected the activities of Kashmiri extremists to focus on the Afghan theater. Of particular note in this regard is LeT, which has long been one of the ISI's most favored strategic assets in the stand-off against India. According to LeT expert Stephen Tankel, the group is now playing a central role in recruiting militants from mosques and madrassas in Peshawar, promising potential fighters both training and subsistence payments for fighting in Afghanistan. Tankel further asserts that the group has redeployed its own cadres to the country and that it has emerged since 2006 as one of several prominent entities battling for control of the contested Korengal Valley in Kunar Province.[21]

Make Pakistan Essential to Afghan Reconciliation Talks

Whereas India had difficulty making itself relevant to Afghan peace negotiations, Islamabad has positioned itself as a vital player in any Afghan political reconciliation process.[22] After NATO attacked a Pakistani border post in November 2011 (an attack that NATO described as unintentional), Pakistan boycotted a multi-national summit meeting held in Bonn the following month to discuss Afghanistan's continued stabilization after the U.S. troop withdrawal.[23] Islamabad's absence was widely seen as undermining the effectiveness of the summit.[24]

Pakistani soil. See Adam Levine, "Panetta Calls Insurgent Attacks in Afghanistan a 'Sign of Weakness,'" CNN, September 22, 2011. See also Matt Waldman, *The Sun in the Sky: The Relationship Between Pakistan's ISI and Afghan Insurgents,* London: London School of Economics and Political Science, Crisis States Research Centre, Working Paper 18, 2010, pp. 1, 21; and Catherine Philip, "Pervez Musharraf Was Playing 'Double Game' with U.S.," *Times,* February 17, 2009.

[18] Dennis Blair, Director of National Intelligence, *Annual Threat Assessment of the US Intelligence Community for the Senate Select Committee on Intelligence,* February 2, 2010, p. 9.

[19] Mark Mazzetti and Eric Schmitt, "Pakistanis Aided Attack in Kabul, U.S. Officials Say," *New York Times,* August 1, 2008.

[20] Abdul Waheed Wafa and Alan Cowell, "Suicide Car Blast Kills 41 in Afghan Capital," *New York Times,* July 8, 2008. See also Sabrina Tavernise and Abdul Waheed Wafa, "17 Die in Kabul Bomb Attack," *New York Times,* October 8, 2009; M. Karim Faiez and Mark Magnier, "Taliban Claims Responsibility for Kabul Embassy Attack," *Los Angeles Times,* October 9, 2009; and Ben Farmer, "Suicide Bombers Target Kabul Hotels Killing Seventeen," *Telegraph,* February 26, 2010.

[21] Stephen Tankel, *Lashkar-e-Taiba: From 9/11 to Mumbai,* London: International Centre for the Study of Radicalisation and Political Violence, April–May 2009, p. 9. See also Alissa Rubin, "Militant Group Expands Attacks in Afghanistan," *New York Times,* June 15, 2010; and Kathy Gannon, "Vengeful New Militant Group Emerges in Pakistan," Associated Press, July 1, 2010.

[22] Verma and Schaffer, 2010.

[23] "Pakistan to Boycott Key Meeting on Afghanistan," Associated Press, November 29, 2011.

[24] Ishaan Tharoor, "The Bonn Conference: Can Afghanistan Be Saved Without Pakistan on Board?" *Time,* December 5, 2011. Despite Pakistan's boycott of the Bonn meeting, Islamabad evidently fears being excluded from important talks

Pakistan has also demonstrated its ability to influence peace negotiations by preventing moderate Taliban figures from participating in talks. This strategy became apparent in February 2010, when, on very short notice, Pakistani authorities seized several senior Taliban leaders across the country, including Abdul Ghani Baradar, Mullah Omar's second in command.[25] Although Washington initially hailed the detentions as a "sea change" in Pakistan's counter-terrorism cooperation with the United States,[26] it appears that the arrests were merely an effort to control the Taliban's political agenda. Most of those taken into custody had reportedly agreed to open talks with the Afghan government and may have been moving to conclude a settlement with Kabul independently of Pakistan.

In addition, Taliban hardliners backed by Pakistan have pledged to undermine the peace process by killing Afghans engaging the Karzai government in reconciliation talks,[27] making clear that only the initiatives they sanction will be permitted to go forward. These extremist elements remain the chief suspects behind the September 2011 and May 2012 assassinations of former Afghan president Burhanuddin Rabbani and former Taliban minister Maulvi Arsala Rahmani—two leading figures in the peace process and both members of the High Peace Council created by President Karzai to engage the Taliban.[28] There is little doubt that the twin killings have impeded the Afghan government's efforts to negotiate an end to the insurgency.

Through its diplomatic initiatives and efforts to limit participation in peace talks led by Kabul, Pakistan has sent three clear messages: (1) it controls who participates in reconciliation talks, (2) it must play a central role in any discussions on ending violence in Afghanistan, and (3) it will obstruct negotiations that do not advance its own interests.[29]

Offer Pakistani Development Aid and Trade to Afghanistan

On the economic front, Pakistan has sought to curry favor in Kabul by extending much-needed development aid to Afghanistan and promoting Afghan exports. The government has spent around $300 million in assistance, most of which has been directed toward the construction of roads and railways[30] that would connect Pakistan to the energy-rich CARs. Islamabad and Kabul signed the Afghanistan–Pakistan Transit Trade Agreement (APTTA), in which Afghanistan would permit Pakistani goods to transit en route to Central Asia, and Pakistan

---

about Afghanistan and does not believe that it can continue shaping negotiations simply by adopting a policy of non-participation. The Pakistani government's decision to reopen Pakistan's borders to NATO materiel entering Afghanistan in May 2012 is widely believed to have been driven by a desire to ensure that Pakistan would be represented in the NATO summit meeting in Chicago scheduled for the following month. See Chris Brummitt, "NATO Invites Pakistan to Summit in Chicago," Associated Press, May 15, 2012.

[25] Ruttig, 2010, p. 6. See also Mark Mazzetti and Dexter Filkins, "Secret Joint Raid Captures Taliban's Top Commander," *New York Times*, February 15, 2010.

[26] See, for instance, Chris Allbritton, "Holbrooke Hails Pakistan–U.S. Collaboration on Taliban," Reuters, February 18, 2010. See also Mazzetti and Filkins, 2010.

[27] "Taliban Flags Start to Spring Fighting Season," 2011.

[28] Laura King, "Former Afghan President Burhanuddin Rabbani Assassinated," *Los Angeles Times*, September 20, 2011; "Afghans Mourn After Killing of Peace Negotiator," Associated Press, May 14, 2012. See also "Gunmen Kill Senior Afghan Peace Negotiator," MSNBC, May 13, 2012.

[29] Ruttig, 2010. See also Coll, 2010; and Verma and Schaffer, 2010. Similar views were expressed to the author during email correspondence with a U.S. security analyst, February 2010.

[30] Afghanistan still lacks a functioning rail system and only recently completed its first significant line—a 75-kilometer track that links the northern city of Mazar-e-Sharif with the city of Hairatan on the border with Uzbekistan.

would allow Afghan products to transit on the way to Indian markets.[31] (Afghan exports to India total about $200 million per year.)[32]

Oppose Afghanistan's Regional Integration

Though Pakistan did not oppose Afghanistan's formal membership in SAARC when it came up for a vote in 2005,[33] Islamabad has otherwise impeded Kabul's political and economic integration into Central and South Asia. The government's reasons for doing so stem from a desire to ensure that its own influence is not diminished and to prevent India from reaping any commercial benefits. As noted, Pakistan has also long blocked two-way Indian-Afghan trade, permitting the latter's goods to cross its territory south but refusing the former's commodities the same access north.[34] (Interestingly, although Pakistan decided on November 2, 2011, to normalize its own bilateral trade with India by granting it most-favored-nation status, Pakistan still continues to block Indian exports to Afghanistan, a fact that suggests that Pakistan is not trying to hurt the Indian economy so much as limit India's access to Afghanistan.)[35]

Secure Central Asian Trade and Energy Resources

As discussed earlier, Pakistan urgently needs to secure foreign imports of oil and gas. The proposed TAPI pipeline would provide as much as 15 percent of Pakistan's current energy consumption. To preserve its ability to procure oil and gas and to otherwise trade with the CARs, Pakistan has pursued a dual-track strategy directed at augmenting cordial regional relations while simultaneously jockeying to box India out. Islamabad has emphasized common historical and religious links to conclude energy deals with such countries as Tajikistan and Kyrgyzstan and has also offered to build road and rail links throughout Central Asia.[36]

Islamabad also seeks to strengthen its trade links with the CARs by controlling both new infrastructure and the Silk Route's traditional western routes that connect Karachi with markets in Uzbekistan, Tajikistan, Kyrgyzstan, and Kazakhstan.[37] Pakistan has secured extensive Chinese assistance to build a port in Gwadar to serve as a gateway for trade with Afghanistan and countries beyond. In addition, through its past support for the Taliban, Pakistan has already assumed a degree of influence over the Kushka-Herat-Kandahar highway, a critical strategic artery that provides the sole non-Iranian trading route between Central Asia and the Indian Ocean and Persian Gulf.

---

[31] Pant, 2011. See also *Agreement Between the Governments of the Islamic Republic of Afghanistan and the Islamic Republic of Pakistan: Afghanistan–Pakistan Transit Trade Agreement, 2010 (APTTA)*, October 28, 2010; Abshire and Browne, 2011, p. 69; and Bajoria, 2009.

[32] "India to Cut Tariff on Imported Goods from Afghanistan," *TOLOnews*, June 6, 2011.

[33] Ijaz Hussain, "Implications of SAARC Enlargement," *Daily Times*, November 23, 2005.

[34] Mukherjee, 2007b, in Bhasin, 2008, p. 1018. See also Pant, 2011; Abshire and Browne, 2011, p. 69; and Bajoria, 2009.

[35] Alex Rodriguez and Mark Magnier, "Pakistan, India Take Another Cautious Step Forward," *Los Angeles Times*, November 7, 2011.

[36] Yossef Bodansky, *Islamabad's Road Warriors*, Houston, Texas: Freeman Center for Strategic Studies, 1995. See also Roy, 2006, p. 802.

[37] The economic importance of this corridor can be measured in terms of revenues lost to smuggling before the Taliban assumed power in Afghanistan. Pakistan's Central Board of Revenue (CBR) reported shortfalls in customs earnings of 3.5 billion rupees in the financial year 1992–1993 and 11 billion rupees during 1994–1995.

Pressure Washington to Protect Pakistani Interests

For a long time, Pakistan has successfully pressured the United States to protect its key strategic interests in Afghanistan, taking advantage of the United States' dependence on Pakistan for counterterrorism cooperation and for permitting transit of supplies destined for U.S. troops in Afghanistan. Islamabad has insisted that Washington minimize India's role in Afghanistan (particularly in the security arena), and it has extracted U.S. military assistance totaling more than $16 billion since 9/11.[38] Indian officials have expressed concern that much of this aid has been redirected from the war on terrorism to support the Pakistani military's anti-Indian posture.[39]

Effectiveness of Pakistan's Strategies

Pakistan has had some measure of success in keeping the Kabul government weak and off-balance. Islamabad's support to the Taliban, particularly the provision of safe haven to the group's leadership, has allowed the insurgency to continue and prevented the Afghan government from asserting its authority over more of Afghanistan. Similarly, Pakistan's efforts to disrupt any attempt at reconciliation in which it is not a key player has undermined Afghan stability and prevented Kabul from developing alliances that Islamabad does not control.

Pakistan has also been able to extend its bilateral trade relations with Afghanistan. Islamabad has managed to enhance overall economic ties with Kabul and currently stands as one of its most important trading partners.[40] The conclusion of the APTTA was also a major boon. Although the agreement had much to do with U.S. backroom lobbying and pressure on Pakistan, Islamabad was able to negotiate terms that enhanced its own commercial links with Afghanistan while limiting India from doing the same—at least in the short term.[41]

For the most part, however, Pakistan's various strategies in Afghanistan have been ineffective. It has failed to prevent Afghanistan's regional integration, expand its own reach into Central Asia, or undermine Indian political and economic influence. Pakistan's failures are largely of its own making. For one, internal rivalries between the civilian leadership and the security institutions prevent a coherent approach to achieving Pakistan's objectives. More importantly, however, some of Pakistan's strategies—particularly its support for jihadists—have backfired by alienating its potential partners in the region and generating internal instability. Pakistan's continuing support for the Haqqani network and other extremists has severely angered the Karzai administration, which has charged that Pakistani border and security units not only

[38] Kronstadt, 2012, p. 38. See also Weinbaum and Harder, 2008, p. 26; Daniel Markey, "A False Choice in Pakistan," *Foreign Affairs*, July–August 2007, p. 88; Sawhney, 2011, p. 11; and Brian Cloughley, "Uneasy Partnership: The US and Pakistan's Dysfunctional Alliance," *Jane's Intelligence Review*, April 14, 2010, p. 8.

[39] D'Souza, 2008, p. 11.

[40] Pakistan is Afghanistan's main export and second-most important import partner (behind the United States). As of 2008, Pakistani exports to Afghanistan were as high as $1.2 billion per year, compared with $25 million during the Taliban's tenure. See Weinbaum and Harder, 2008, p. 27.

[41] Pant, 2011. See also Abshire and Browne, 2011, p. 69. Although the APTTA permits Afghan exports to India to transit Pakistani territory, it does not allow the reverse flow (currently, Indian exports to Afghanistan have to go via Iran). It should also be noted that Washington's long-term objective is to fully integrate Delhi into the APTTA, which would eventually stymie Islamabad's current relative advantage in terms of two-way trade with Kabul.

lack the capacity but, more intrinsically, the will to stem cross-border infiltration.[42] Relations have become so tense at times that Karzai has even threatened to send troops across the border to attack militants operating from bases in Islamabad's tribal belt.[43] These policies have so undermined Pakistani ties with Afghanistan, one Pakistani newspaper asserted, that "our brilliant strategists have succeeded beyond measure in driving Afghanistan into the arms of India."[44]

The heightened level of mistrust between the Afghan and Pakistani governments has played directly to India's advantage, helping to deepen the Kabul–Delhi partnership.[45] This was clearly in evidence following the 2008 suicide attack on the Indian embassy in Kabul. In the aftermath of the incident, Afghan Foreign Minister Rangeen Dadfar Spanta issued a statement declaring that such attacks by the "enemy" would do nothing to harm his country's deep relationship with India.[46] President Karzai later went on to identify exactly who he believed the enemy was: "[T]he killings of people in Afghanistan, the destruction of bridges in Afghanistan . . . are carried out by Pakistan's intelligence and Pakistan's military departments."[47]

To some extent, Pakistan has succeeded at making itself seemingly indispensable to the United States. Although it has provided valuable counterterrorism assistance, it has also provided support to anti-American insurgents, thereby extending the conflict and ensuring that Pakistan remains relevant to U.S. policymakers.[48] However, Islamabad's use of surrogates in Afghanistan has, on the whole, substantially complicated its ties with the United States. Tensions became especially acute after the Haqqani network's September 13, 2011, assault on the U.S. embassy in Kabul, an attack that senior U.S. officials publicly asserted was conducted with ISI support.[49] Exasperation over Islamabad's backing of insurgents who routinely target U.S. forces and its provision of safe haven to Taliban fighters has led many in Congress on both sides of the aisle to question the wisdom of continuing to support Pakistan. Indeed, in July 2011, the Obama administration announced that it was temporarily suspending $800 million in planned security aid for Pakistan, around one-third of the annual total that had been earmarked for Pakistan.[50]

Furthermore, Pakistan's unwillingness to take concerted action against Islamists who find safe haven inside Pakistani territory has undermined one of Pakistan's primary claims to relevance in U.S. anti-terrorist initiatives: the notion that its territory, and thus its cooperation, is absolutely necessary to eliminating the Taliban, the Haqqani network, LeT, and other extremists hostile to both the United States and India. Many U.S. officials assert that, as long

---

[42] Cloughley, 2010, p. 10.

[43] Wafa and Cowell, 2008.

[44] "Indo-Afghan Strategic Partnership," 2011.

[45] See, for instance, Tellis, 2011, p. 1.

[46] Sardar Ahmad, "28 Killed in Suicide Attack at India's Afghanistan Embassy," Agence France-Presse, July 7, 2008.

[47] Sayed Salahuddin, "Karzai Says Pakistan Behind Indian Embassy Bomb," Reuters, July 14, 2008.

[48] Krasner, 2012.

[49] Joint Chiefs Chairman Admiral Mike Mullen testified to the Senate Armed Services Committee on September 22, 2011, that, "with ISI support, Haqqani operatives planned and conducted that truck bomb attack [that wounded 77 NATO troops on September 10, 2011], as well as the assault on our embassy." See Elisabeth Bumiller and Jane Perlez, "Pakistan's Spies Linked to Raid on US Embassy," *Boston Globe*, September 23, 2011.

[50] "In a Sulk: Relations Grow Yet Worse Between Pakistan and the Superpower," *Economist*, July 14, 2011.

as these groups can regroup, train, acquire funds, and procure supplies inside Pakistan, U.S. strategy in Afghanistan will be severely complicated and terrorist threats to the United States will never be eliminated.[51] However, Islamabad's failure to establish state control in the FATA and eliminate these safe havens over the course of the past decade—despite billions of dollars in U.S. military assistance—has demonstrated that Pakistani cooperation toward this goal has not been productive. Indeed, it appears to be official Pakistani policy to protect such safe havens, given that, as has been discussed, Islamabad has long seen the groups that take refuge there as strategic assets in Pakistan's national security arsenal.

Apart from fraying its relations with Afghanistan and the United States, Pakistan's partnership with jihadists has backfired, as some of the groups have turned on their sponsor. For the past decade, the Pakistani government and security institutions have attempted to differentiate between "good" jihadists, who help pressure India and extend Pakistani influence in Afghanistan, and "bad" jihadists, who collaborate with al Qaeda, use terrorism to pursue global objectives, or create instability within Pakistan.[52] However, such simple dichotomies have not played out in reality. Such groups as JeM and HuM have splintered, with new factions emerging that have been tied to bombings and assassinations within Pakistan, including at least two attempts on the life of then-president Pervez Musharraf.[53]

Furthermore, groups in the tribal areas that once played a leading role in the Afghan insurgency, angered by Islamabad's collaboration with Washington, have reconfigured as the Tehrik-e-Taliban Pakistan (TTP), which devotes all its energies inward against the Pakistani state.[54] Moreover, there is evidence to suggest that both pro- and anti-Islamabad Islamists enjoy a close operational and logistical relationship—something that reflects their common affinity with radical Pashtun madrassas connected to the Jamiat Ulema-e-Islam (JUI)—and have been prepared to share intelligence, money, and even suicide cadres.[55] In addition to threatening the government's grip on power, the resulting instability undermines Pakistan's standing in the international community and renders the country a less hospitable place for foreign investment.

Pakistan's efforts to establish trade links in Central Asia have been equally unsuccessful. Although the government has moved to establish cordial relations and has concluded some energy deals, many Central Asian states remain highly wary of Islamabad's overtures and intentions. This reticence stems in large part from past and present ISI support for domestic extremist organizations—including the Islamic Movement of Uzbekistan (IMU) and the United Tajik Opposition (UTO)—a policy that again aims to use proxies as a means for gain-

---

[51] Secretary of Defense Leon Panetta, for example, said in June that "it is difficult to achieve a secure Afghanistan as long as there is a safe haven for terrorists in Pakistan from which they can conduct attacks on our forces." See John Bentley, "Leon Panetta: U.S. 'Reaching the Limits of Our Patience' with Pakistan Terror Safe Havens," CBS News, June 7, 2012.

[52] Fair and Chalk, 2006, p. 68. See also Markey, 2007. See also Pir Zubair Shah and Carlotta Gall, "For Pakistan, Deep Ties to Militant Network May Trump U.S. Pressure," *New York Times*, October 31, 2011.

[53] The attempted assassinations were carried out in 2003 by a group calling itself the Jamaat ul-Furqun—a splinter faction of JeM.

[54] The TTP's current leadership has made no secret of its intention to destroy the present government in Islamabad as part of a broader, united Islamist onslaught on both sides of the Pakistan–Afghanistan border. See Ron Moreau and Sabrina Taversine, "The End of al Qaeda?" *Newsweek*, August 7, 2009.

[55] Shah and Gall, 2011.

ing greater leverage over regimes in the region.[56] Just as in Afghanistan, pursuing such a course has strained Pakistan's bilateral relations with these countries and undermined the potential for trade, particularly given that they can access alternative road infrastructure and maritime outlets (notably, in Iran and Turkey) and thus do not require access to Pakistani territory. Pakistan's efforts to develop a port at Gwadar that would facilitate China's access to Central Asia have been relatively unsuccessful, both because of the continued instability of Afghanistan, which goods would have to cross, and because of the existence of alternative port facilities.

Unlike India, Pakistan has failed to leverage its $300 million in development assistance to improve its image in Afghanistan.[57] Pakistani assistance is a mere quarter of the $1.3 billion provided to date by India, giving Pakistan's projects much less visibility than its rival's. As Pakistani journalist Yousafzai Rahimullah has written, Pakistan "failed to build a hospital, college, or road that could serve as a visible example of Pakistan's generosity towards Afghanistan."[58] In sharp contrast to India, therefore, Pakistan has been unable to project soft power successfully in Afghanistan.

Islamabad has also failed to exclude Delhi from the region. From the point of view of Central Asian governments, India has more to offer in terms of economic links and export markets, is transparent and consistent in its strategic objectives, and is not tainted by association with hostile Islamist militants. Furthermore, Central Asian states have few concerns that Indian power projection will threaten their interests or lead to instability in the region.[59] In virtually all respects, therefore, the CARs view Delhi as a more valuable and reliable partner than Islamabad, a dynamic that makes it harder for Pakistan to negotiate competitive trade and energy agreements in Central Asia.

Finally, Pakistan's multiple centers of power have made it difficult for the country to formulate a coherent policy that advances its strategic interests. The leadership of the army, including that of the ISI—which collectively calls most of the shots in Pakistan—views Afghanistan primarily as an extension of Pakistan's conflict with India. This worldview has effectively eliminated any latitude to develop strategies and policies that could generate more comprehensive benefits for Pakistan. As Frédéric Grare observed,

> Pakistan has managed to turn almost every other dimension of its regional policy—such as its dispute with Afghanistan regarding the border issue and Pashtunistan, and its dealings with Central Asia and the United States—into a zero-sum game with India.[60]

[56] Roy, 2006, pp. 807–808, 818–819. See also Vinod Anand, "Pakistan as a Factor in Afghan Stability," in R. K. Sawhney, Arun Sahgal, and Gurmeet Kanwal, eds., *Afghanistan: A Role for India*, New Delhi: Centre for Land Warfare Studies, 2011, p. 159. For insights on how such Central Asian Islamist groups as the IMU and JUI received support from both the Pakistani-backed Taliban and Pakistan's ISI Directorate, see Peter Sinnott, "Peeling the Waziristan Onion: Central Asians in Armed Islamist Movements in Afghanistan and Pakistan," *China and Eurasia Forum Quarterly*, Vol. 7, No. 4, 2009, pp. 37, 41–45, 50. See also Ahmed Rashid, "The Taliban: Exporting Extremism," *Foreign Affairs*, Vol. 78, No. 6, November–December 1999, pp. 26–27. See also Didier Chaudet, "Islamist Terrorism in Greater Central Asia: The 'al-Qaedaization' of Uzbek Jihadism," *Russia.Nie.Visions*, No. 35, December 2008, pp. 11–12.

[57] Wax, 2010.

[58] Yousafzai Rahimullah, "Pakistan's Loss in Afghanistan Is India's Gain," *News*, July 13, 2003, as quoted in Ijaz Khan, *Pakistan's Strategic Culture and Foreign Policy Making: A Study of Pakistan's Post 9/11 Afghan Policy Change*, New York: Nova Science Publishers, 2007, p. 71.

[59] Roy, 2006, p. 822.

[60] Grare, 2010, p. 17.

Pakistan's civilian leadership, which may well be interested in pursuing a more comprehensive strategy that advances the country's bilateral relations and energy-related interests with key partners, is marginalized and currently has little influence to develop a more balanced policy vis-à-vis Afghanistan. In other words, the India-centric approach of the ISI and the military has directly undermined Pakistan's ability to achieve its broader national goals.

CHAPTER FOUR
Afghanistan

In considering how India and Pakistan will pursue their interests in Afghanistan, it is necessary to consider how Afghanistan defines and pursues its own interests and how it will react to steps taken by its neighbors. Afghanistan may be the least powerful of the three countries, even regarding its own fate, but it is not a passive actor. In fact, President Hamid Karzai has been remarkably successful in balancing his outreach to, and pressure from, his country's two more powerful partners.

Afghanistan's Strategic Objectives

The Karzai administration's core objective, above all else, is to maintain its power and influence. After years in exile and a decade of trying to rebuild their state virtually from scratch, few senior Afghan officials are inclined to step down. Perhaps more significantly, given that Afghanistan is assessed to be one of the most corrupt countries in the world,[1] it is equally as unlikely that these individuals would willingly walk away from positions that guarantee them power, influence, and a great deal of money. Thus, although Karzai claims that he will step down—as required by the Afghan constitution—at the close of his second term in 2014,[2] it is entirely plausible that he will seek changes to the constitution that would allow him to remain in office. If he does not, or if such an effort proves politically infeasible, members of his inner circle will doubtless maintain some degree of influence in government and commerce.

Other than maintaining its own position, the Karzai administration has several overarching policy objectives. First, it seeks to increase central government control over the country, a task that will be increasingly difficult once the U.S. military withdraws. Neither the army nor the police force is especially capable, and it is doubtful that either will be able to exert authority in areas where even U.S. troops have failed to do so. Karzai (or his successor) may therefore have a considerable incentive to solicit additional assistance from India. A reinvigorated Indian economic aid and reconstruction program could help the Kabul government continue to build popular support. Continued Indian military and police training would make Afghan security forces more effective in countering the Taliban and other Pakistani-backed insurgents; this training initiative would be even more successful if Delhi were to send instructors to Afghanistan in order to increase the number of Afghan security forces who could receive training.

---

[1] In 2011, Transparency International ranked Afghanistan as the fourth-most corrupt country in the world, behind only Somalia, North Korea, and Myanmar. See Transparency International, *Corruption Perceptions Index 2011*, 2011, pp. 4–5.

[2] Ben Farmer, "Hamid Karzai Says He Will Not Seek Third Term," *Telegraph*, August 11, 2011.

To truly consolidate central government control, Karzai must outmaneuver his two most significant internal threats—the Pashtun Taliban and the non-Pashtun opposition parties made up of former NA figures. Although his success will depend on a wide range of domestic factors, Pakistan and India will figure significantly into his calculations. Karzai will have little chance of cutting the Taliban off from its Pakistani lifeline unless he is able to reduce poppy cultivation, rein in corruption, and gain some measure of control over the border with Pakistan—all Herculean tasks. However, Karzai will attempt to co-opt the Taliban through the reconciliation process, working diligently to ensure that Washington advocates his own positions while engaging factions of the Taliban that are minimally beholden to Pakistan, and hoping that granting a modest but not decisive role in the central government to such elements of the Taliban will cause the insurgency to wane.

It will be difficult for Karzai to marginalize non-Pashtun factions, as ethnic Tajiks occupy senior positions throughout the national security apparatus[3] and an outsized proportion of the Afghan National Army's officer and non-commissioned officer corps.[4] It is likely that, as part of broader arrangements with India, Karzai will try to extract from Delhi a concession that it will not provide any support to its erstwhile proxies that would undercut his administration.

Second, Karzai will continue working to counter Pakistani influence in Afghanistan by drawing closer to Delhi in a wide range of areas. In the Indo-Afghan Strategic Partnership Agreement signed in October 2011, Karzai secured Indian commitments for high-level political consultations; extensive investment in Afghanistan's mining, energy, communication, and transportation sectors; education and training assistance; an additional $500 million in reconstruction and development aid; and, most significantly, training for the ANSF and Afghan National Police.[5]

Third, President Karzai will need to improve the economy if he is to increase his legitimacy among the wider Afghan population.[6] The Afghan government will make every effort to continue its development and growth through foreign aid—currently 91 percent of the licit Afghan economy, according to the World Bank[7]—and private investment. As already discussed, India will be a much more important contributor to Afghanistan's reconstruction and economic growth than Pakistan will be, a fact that will drive Kabul to forge closer economic ties with Delhi. Eager for additional investment, Afghanistan will also likely pursue investment and trade deals with China, Iran, and Russia despite likely opposition from Delhi (which wants to avoid further inroads by Beijing), Islamabad (which wants to minimize Iranian and Russian influence in Afghanistan), and Washington (which would prefer to see Kabul exclude all three).

---

[3]   Selig S. Harrison, "Afghanistan's Tyranny of the Minority," *New York Times*, August 16, 2009.

[4]   Obaid Younossi, Peter Dahl Thruelsen, Jonathan Vaccaro, Jerry M. Sollinger, and Brian Grady, *The Long March: Building an Afghan National Army*, Santa Monica, Calif.: RAND Corporation, MG-845-RDCC/OSD, 2009, p. 22.

[5]   Ministry of External Affairs, India, "Joint Declaration Between India and Afghanistan on the Occasion of the Visit of the Prime Minister of India," May 12, 2011.

[6]   Pant, 2010a, p. 138.

[7]   Robert B. Zoellick, "Afghanistan's Biggest Need: A Flourishing Economy," *Washington Post*, July 22, 2011. Afghanistan's illicit opium revenues represent as much as one-quarter of Afghanistan's total economic activity. See Christopher M. Blanchard, *Afghanistan: Narcotics and U.S. Policy*, Washington, D.C.: Congressional Research Service, RL32686, August 12, 2009, p. 3.

Afghanistan's Strategies vis-à-vis India and Pakistan

Karzai has been remarkably successful in harnessing—some might say manipulating—both India and Pakistan to advance Afghanistan's primary geopolitical and economic objectives. For example, Karzai has managed to reduce Afghanistan's reliance on Pakistani territory for trade and to erode (at least to some degree) Pakistan's influence over Afghan affairs by building ties to India, by shaping the reconciliation process, and by participating in U.S.-led COIN operations. Yet, at the same time, Karzai downplays the significance of such cooperation in statements aimed at assuaging Pakistan's concerns and takes other steps to encourage Islamabad to see the benefits of collaborating with, rather than subverting, his government.

Remarkably, President Karzai has managed to secure large-scale Indian aid and investment without causing Islamabad to retaliate by undermining his regime or stirring up even greater unrest. (One could claim that Pakistani-sponsored attacks on Indian diplomatic posts in Afghanistan were exceptions to this achievement.) Key to his success has been his adept balancing of his outreach to both countries. One day after India agreed to train Afghan security forces in the landmark October 2011 Indo-Afghan Strategic Partnership Agreement, Karzai offered reassurances that the agreement "is not directed against any country" and called Pakistan his nation's "twin brother."[8] Then, just one month later, he agreed to accept Pakistan's offer of military training for Afghan forces, made at a multi-national summit held in Istanbul.[9]

Similarly, even as Karzai has worked to minimize Pakistani influence in his country, he has moderated his criticism of Islamabad with counterbalancing praise. Thus, in October 2011—merely a day after denouncing Islamabad for harboring terrorists (while standing alongside U.S. Secretary of State Hillary Clinton)—Karzai again stated that "Pakistan is a brother" and asserted that his country would side with it in the event of war with India or the United States.[10] While Karzai fights back against Pakistani interference, he wraps his fists in velvet gloves.

In playing India against Pakistan, Karzai is following a well-trodden path of Afghan leaders who have sought to balance Afghanistan's two more powerful South Asian neighbors. Opposed to the inclusion of Pashtun areas in the NWFP in post-colonial Pakistan, Afghanistan rejected the validity of the British-demarcated Durand Line in 1949, leading to years of Afghan support for Pashtun and Baloch secessionism and cordial relations with India (which supported Afghan irredentist claims)[11] under prime minister (1953–1963) and later president (1973–1978) Mohammed Daoud Khan. Yet, under King Zahir Shah, Kabul supported Pakistan during the 1965 and 1971 Indo-Pakistan wars, demonstrating to the Pakistani government that Afghanistan can serve as an ally during a crisis.[12]

[8] "Pakistan Our Twin Brother, India a Great Friend: Hamid Karzai," *Times of India*, October 5, 2011.

[9] Mariana Baabar, "Pakistan to Train Afghan Troops," *International News*, November 4, 2011.

[10] Ray Rivera and Sangar Rahimi, "Afghan President Says His Country Would Back Pakistan in a Clash with the U.S.," *New York Times*, October 23, 2011. See also Lydia Polgreen, "Karzai Tries to Soothe Pakistan over Warmer Relations with India," *New York Times*, October 5, 2011.

[11] Chris Alexander, "Afghanistan and Pakistan: A Strategy for Peace," *Options Politiques*, November 2010, p. 30. See also Ganguly and Howenstein, 2009, pp. 127–128; and Hasan-Askari Rizvi, *Pakistan's Foreign Policy: An Overview 1947–2004*, Pakistan Institute of Legislative Development and Transparency, Briefing Paper 11, April 2004, p. 10.

[12] Riaz M. Khan, *Afghanistan and Pakistan: Conflict, Extremism, and Resistance to Modernity*, Washington, D.C.: Woodrow Wilson Center Press, 2011, p. 166.

Similarly, in seeking good relations with a wide range of extra-regional parties—such as the United States, Iran, Russia, and China—Karzai is only the latest Afghan leader to seek to extract concessions from multiple outside powers, including hostile ones. As historian Thomas Barfield writes,

> In a country that often cultivated a reputation for isolation and xenophobia, Afghan leaders had always proved remarkably shrewd in dealing with the outside world. Historically they negotiated even with their worst enemies if they thought they could come to a useful accommodation.[13]

Thus, with the British kept more or less at bay in the wake of the second Anglo-Afghan War and a territorial agreement in the form of the Durand Line, King Nadir Shah concluded a non-aggression pact with the Soviet Union in the early 1930s as a way of keeping Afghanistan's northern neighbor out of its affairs. Despite this agreement, his son and successor, Zahir Shah, sought patrons from outside the region—particularly Germany, Japan, and the United States—to balance Soviet pressure.[14]

Later, in the years immediately following Indian and Pakistani independence, Afghanistan tried to take advantage of the U.S.–Soviet rivalry, seeking, as Barfield writes, "to warm Afghanistan with the heat generated by the great power conflicts without getting drawn into them directly."[15] The Afghan government sought military assistance and recognition of its claims to Pashtunistan from the United States, in part to balance increasing Soviet interest in Afghanistan. However, after the Harry S. Truman administration urged Kabul to drop its claims to Pashtunistan in 1951, and after the Dwight D. Eisenhower administration approved arms sales to Pakistan while rejecting Afghanistan's requests for military aid in 1954, Prime Minister Daoud immediately turned to Moscow, which offered military assistance, development aid, and support for Afghan's territorial claims.[16] In the subsequent three decades, Washington and Moscow competed for influence in Afghanistan by providing more than $1 billion of foreign aid, which made up as much as 89 percent of the Afghan government's budget.[17]

Although President Karzai will continue this traditional Afghan strategy of pursuing national objectives by striking a balance between more powerful foreign nations, overall, it is clear that Afghanistan stands to gain more from consolidating ties with Delhi than from doing so with Islamabad. Although Pakistan is a valuable trading partner simply by virtue of its location, it has little to contribute in the way of investment, regional integration, or assistance with economic and political development. Indeed, the closer Islamabad gets to Kabul, the more of a destabilizing influence it is likely to have. India, by contrast, has much more to

---

[13] Thomas J. Barfield, *Afghanistan: A Cultural and Political History*, Princeton, N.J.: Princeton University Press, 2010, p. 221.

[14] Barfield, 2010, pp. 153–154, 205.

[15] Barfield, 2010, p. 206.

[16] Leon B. Poullada, "Afghanistan and the United States: The Crucial Years," *Middle East Journal*, Vol. 35, No. 2, Spring 1981, pp. 182–184, 186–189. See also Barnett R. Rubin, *The Fragmentation of Afghanistan: State Formation and Collapse in the International System*, New Haven, Conn.: Yale University Press, 2002, p. 65.

[17] Richard F. Nyrop and Donald M. Seekins, eds., *Afghanistan: A Country Study*, Washington, D.C.: Federal Research Division, Library of Congress, January 1986, pp. 146–147.

offer Afghanistan in terms of development aid, constructive security assistance, and help with fostering profitable regional economic integration.

CHAPTER FIVE

Implications for the United States

Try as it might, the United States will never be able to "balance" its relations with India and Pakistan because both sides are annoyed by U.S. ties with the other. Islamabad chafes at Washington's trade and military links, civilian nuclear cooperation, and recently signed "strategic partnership" with Delhi. For its part, India views U.S. counterterrorism collaboration with Pakistan as an augmentation of Pakistan's military capabilities and thus a potential threat to India's security. Although senior U.S. officials have denied that interaction with either of the two countries is a "zero-sum" game, the perception that this is the case persists nevertheless. Efforts to strike a balance between the two will lead the United States to be held "hostage to the vicissitudes of India-Pakistan relations."[1]

Implications for U.S. Policy Toward Afghanistan

Among the more critical U.S. goals for Afghanistan are promoting stability and long-term political and economic development, integrating Afghanistan into the regional economy, developing capable and self-reliant Afghan security forces, defeating the Taliban-led insurgency, and reaching an Afghan-led political settlement that will isolate al Qaeda and Taliban fighters committed to violence, prevent return of that violence, and enhance regional stability.[2] Many of the Pakistani government's most fundamental goals for Afghanistan—particularly a weak regime in Kabul that is open to its influence, a permissive environment in which extremist groups can operate, and the minimization of Indian political and economic influence—are inconsistent with these U.S. objectives. Indeed, as discussed, Pakistan is already providing material support to the Taliban, enabling its safe havens, and advocating for it in reconciliation talks. Islamabad could continue on this path—thereby prolonging the civil war in Afghanistan—if it believes that its interests there will be threatened. This does not necessarily make Islamabad an adversary, but it does suggest that Pakistan is not going to help advance long-term U.S. strategic interests in Afghanistan and that continuing to accommodate Pakistan's fears of growing Indian influence will generate few benefits.

---

[1] Tellis, 2008, p. 36.

[2] Daniel F. Feldman, deputy special representative for Afghanistan and Pakistan, U.S. Department of State, testimony before the U.S. House of Representatives Committee on Foreign Affairs, Subcommittee on the Middle East and South Asia, April 5, 2011, pp. 27–31. See also "White Paper of the Interagency Policy Group's Report on U.S. Policy Toward Afghanistan and Pakistan," undated; and Barack Obama, "Remarks of President Barack Obama on the Way Forward in Afghanistan," Washington, D.C.: White House, June 22, 2011.

In contrast, India would appear to be a far more constructive and reliable long-term partner for the United States in Afghanistan. Delhi and Washington share critical objectives in Afghanistan, including bringing stability and economic growth to the country and preventing the Taliban from gaining influence. The two countries also consider themselves to be prime targets of Pakistani-backed Islamist militants, and both urgently seek to eliminate these entities and their supporters from the region. Although Washington is almost certainly concerned that India's collaboration with Iran on regional trade may improve Tehran's ability to sway events in Afghanistan, this same partnership has the ancillary benefit of helping to reduce China's influence in the region.

The United States would thus be better off attempting to drive events in Afghanistan by promoting an active Indian role to fill the security and economic vacuum created by the drawdown of U.S. troops—even if Pakistan responds by continuing to block U.S. supply convoys and by ramping up its support for the Taliban, which could exacerbate the insurgency in the near term. As previously noted, Delhi's objectives and ability to project power in the Afghanistan are in line with basic U.S. objectives, whereas Pakistan's goals and efforts to exert influence are not; as a result, India has a far greater potential to contribute to Afghanistan's stability and growth than Pakistan does. In short, an active Indian role would increase India's physical and economic security while also helping to preserve and advance the U.S. contribution to Afghan security and reconstruction.

The United States has already promoted an active Indian role in Afghanistan in the economic arena and generally welcomes Delhi's contributions to reconstruction, capacity-building, and development efforts in the country.[3] In October 2011, Washington's Special Representative for Afghanistan and Pakistan, Marc Grossman, discussed ways to further increase Indian investment with senior officials in Delhi, indicating that both sides see mutual benefit from continuing in this direction.[4]

As early as 2010, it was U.S. policy to encourage greater regional economic engagement in Afghanistan as a way to shift "the calculus of Afghanistan's neighbors from competition in Afghanistan to cooperation and economic integration."[5] The May 2012 U.S.–Afghanistan Strategic Partnership Agreement further defined this strategy by calling for expanded regional investment, infrastructure construction, and trade agreements "to enhance regional stability and prosperity [by] restoring Afghanistan's historic role as a bridge connecting Central and South Asia and the Middle East."[6]

Multiple U.S. officials have specified that India, in particular, has a critical role to play in this regard. In September 2011, for instance, Secretary of State Hillary Clinton launched the U.S. vision for a "New Silk Road" in which South and Central Asian countries would help

[3]   For example, White House, "Joint Statement by President Obama and Prime Minister Singh of India," press release, November 8, 2010. See also U.S. Department of State, "U.S.–India Strategic Dialogue Joint Statement," media note, June 3, 2010.

[4]   "U.S. AfPak Envoy Backs Indian Investment in Afghanistan, Strategic Pact," Indo Asian News Service, October 12, 2011.

[5]   Office of the Special Representative for Afghanistan and Pakistan, U.S. Department of State, *Afghanistan and Pakistan Regional Stabilization Strategy*, Washington, D.C., updated February 2010, p. ii.

[6]   Enduring Strategic Partnership Agreement Between the United States of America and the Islamic Republic of Afghanistan, 2012, ¶ IV(3).

Afghans prosper by creating jobs, thereby undercutting the appeal of extremism.[7] To implement such an initiative, as Assistant Secretary of State Robert Blake explained a week later, Afghanistan's neighbors would "promote private-sector investment, increase regional trade and transit, and foster a network of linkages throughout the region." India, Blake asserted, would be "an anchor of the New Silk Road."[8]

Implications for U.S. Policy Toward India

The United States has, under both the George W. Bush and Obama administrations, approached India as a strategic partner that has much to offer the United States over the long term. As the world's largest democracy, a fast-growing economy with extensive commercial links to the United States and throughout Asia, and a rising military power with aspirations to contribute to stability in the Indian Ocean and elsewhere, strategic collaboration with India has the potential to advance multiple U.S. geopolitical objectives. Indeed, Assistant Secretary Blake told Congress in April 2011 that "a strategy of sustained, multi-faceted engagement with India contributes to stability and security in the United States, the South Asia region, and the world" and that "the global strategic partnership with India will remain among our top foreign policy priorities."[9]

Although U.S.–Indian relations have so far been mostly focused on bilateral, rather than regional, issues,[10] a closer partnership on Afghanistan could bode well for collaboration on other global challenges as well. As South Asia scholar Teresita Schaffer writes,

> In the coming decades, as both countries grapple with problems that demand a global solution, the regional and global dimension of their ties will need to grow. . . . In particular, the U.S. sees India as a nascent great power that could help counter Chinese influence in Asia.[11]

Indian academic C. Raja Mohan makes a similar point in a 2006 article for *Foreign Affairs*, writing,

> A rising India may be difficult at times, but it will act broadly to defend and promote the many interests it shares with Washington. Assisting India's rise, then, is in the United States' own long-term interest.[12]

---

[7] Hillary Clinton, Secretary of State, "Remarks at the New Silk Road Ministerial Meeting," New York, September 22, 2011b.

[8] Robert O. Blake Jr., assistant secretary, Bureau of South and Central Asian Affairs, U.S. Department of State, "Looking Ahead: U.S.–India Strategic Relations and the Transpacific Century," remarks, National Bureau of Asian Research, Washington, D.C., September 28, 2011c.

[9] Robert O. Blake Jr., assistant secretary, Bureau of South and Central Asian Affairs, U.S. Department of State, testimony before the U.S. House of Representatives Committee on Foreign Affairs, Subcommittee on the Middle East and South Asia, April 5, 2011b, pp. 9, 11.

[10] Teresita C. Schaffer, *India and the United States in the 21st Century: Reinventing Partnership*, Washington, D.C.: Center for Strategic and International Studies Press, 2009, p. 2.

[11] Schaffer, 2009, pp. 2, 12. Also see George W. Bush, *The National Security Strategy*, Washington, D.C.: White House, March 2006.

[12] C. Raja Mohan, "India and the Balance of Power," *Foreign Affairs*, July–August 2006, p. 32.

Implications for U.S. Policy Toward Pakistan

It is likely that Pakistan would view U.S. efforts to promote a strong Indian role in Afghanistan as nothing short of treachery, and Islamabad would doubtless do all it could to undermine such a policy. Most notably, Pakistan could retaliate against the United States for encouraging greater Indian involvement by undermining the Afghan reconciliation process, which Washington hopes will facilitate a timely U.S. military withdrawal by mitigating the potential for a resumption of widespread violence. Islamabad has already demonstrated that it is willing to obstruct or even scuttle the peace process when its principal political objective—a significant role for pro-Pakistani Taliban in the Afghan political system—is threatened, and it could conceivably derail negotiations again if it felt that other strategic interests were imperiled.

In addition, Pakistan could obstruct the delivery of non-lethal supplies to U.S. forces in Afghanistan, 40 percent of which currently flow through Pakistani territory. It could also limit access to ground lines of communication through Pakistan when NATO withdraws its forces and equipment from Afghanistan in 2014, which the commander of the U.S. Transportation Command, General William Fraser, told a Senate committee in February 2012 would greatly complicate the drawdown.[13]

Islamabad did, in fact, close its Afghan border crossing to NATO convoys following an attack on Pakistani frontier posts in November 2011, a move that greatly increased U.S.–Pakistani tensions. The dispute came to a head six months later, when Pakistani president Asif Ali Zardari was invited to attend the May 2012 NATO summit in Chicago on the expectation that he would announce the reopening of the border, only to have the deal collapse over a disagreement regarding the fees to be paid. Even though the cost of shipping goods through the far longer NDN (depicted in Figure 5.1) is $100 million per month higher than the cost of shipping through Pakistan, Secretary of Defense Leon Panetta stated that the United States refused on principle "to get gouged on the price" by Pakistan.[14] After Secretary of State Clinton issued a carefully worded apology for the November 2011 incident, Pakistan agreed on July 3, 2012, to reopen the border without imposing any fees.[15]

Future Pakistani obstructionism is unlikely to have as significant an impact on U.S. policy as many commentators believe[16] because Washington's dependence on Pakistan is oversold and impermanent. Pakistan seeks a pliable, Taliban-dominated regime in Kabul that would permit a continued safe haven for anti-Indian extremists, a goal that is inconsistent with U.S. objectives. Islamabad has no reason to facilitate an Afghan reconciliation process that advances U.S. objectives at the expense of its own, even if the United States were to again ask India to minimize its engagement in Afghanistan; as noted, the Pakistani government would prefer to derail

---

[13] Nathan Hodge, "U.S. Secures New Afghan Exit Routes," *Wall Street Journal*, February 29, 2012, p. 17.

[14] Karen DeYoung, "Pakistan Border Closure Costs U.S. $100 Million a Month," *Washington Post*, June 13, 2012; Anita Joshua, "Bickering Still on over NATO Lines," *The Hindu*, May 28, 2012. For a discussion of the NDN, see Andrew C. Kuchins and Thomas M. Sanderson, *The Northern Distribution Network and Afghanistan: Geopolitical Challenges and Opportunities—A Report of the CSIS Transnational Threats Project and the Russia and Eurasia Program*, Washington, D.C.: Center for Strategic and International Studies, January 2010.

[15] Bradley Klapper and Rebecca Santana, "US Says Sorry, Pakistan Opens Afghan Supply Lines," Associated Press, July 3, 2012.

[16] For the argument that Washington should refrain from "getting tough" with Pakistan because it will depend on Pakistani influence in Afghanistan in the future, see Robert Dreyfuss, "Like It or Not, America Needs Pakistan," *Inquirer*, November 30, 2011.

Figure 5.1
Afghanistan Supply Routes: Northern Distribution Network and Pakistan Overland Routes

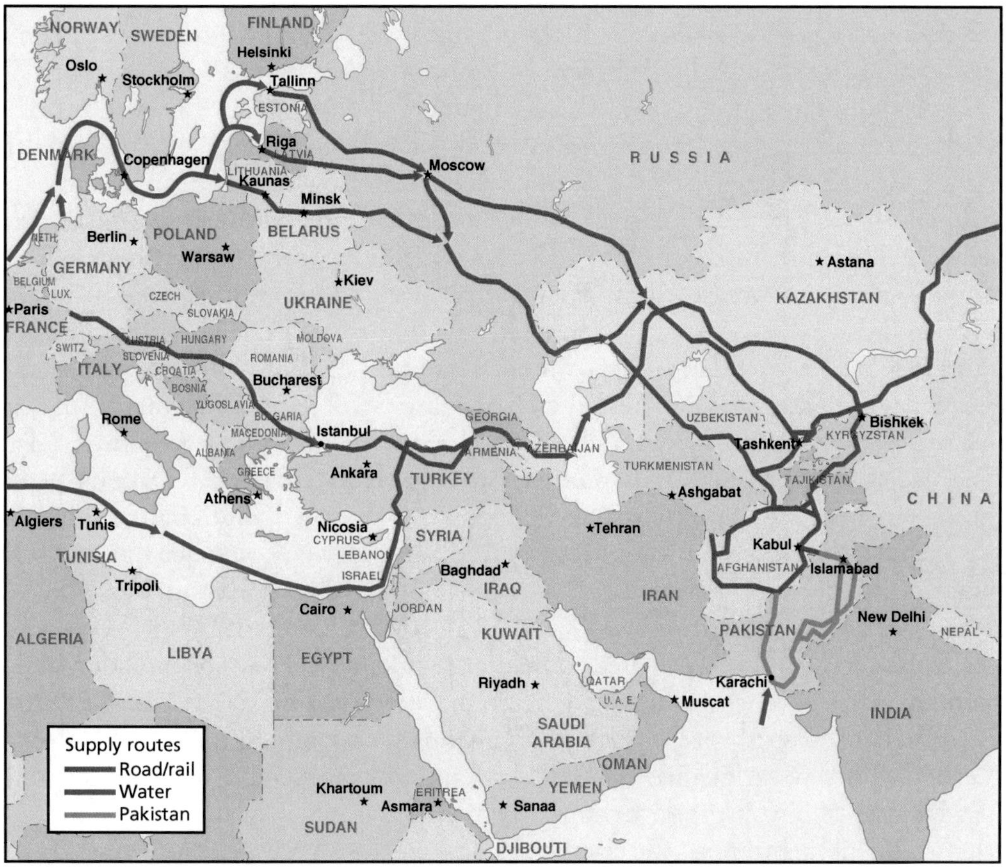

SOURCE: U.S. Transportation Command, 2011.
RAND OP387-5.1

talks entirely. The United States is therefore not dependent on Pakistani cooperation to achieve a political settlement in Afghanistan; in fact, the opposite is true: If Washington does secure a negotiated agreement that marginalizes pro-Pakistan Taliban elements, it will have done so in spite of Pakistani opposition.

Furthermore, though Pakistani supply routes are important to U.S. forces in Afghanistan, alternatives exist. The United States developed the NDN to avoid being dependent on a single supply line—particularly one populated by insurgents and controlled by a government suspicious of U.S. policy—to support its troops in Afghanistan.[17] The NDN could also be used to facilitate the eventual withdrawal of materiel and troops from Afghanistan because the

---

[17] NATO as a whole reduced its dependence on Pakistani supply lines from 80 percent of non-lethal supplies to 40–50 percent by November 2011, and it has stockpiled supplies to mitigate the impact of future Pakistani border closings and of frequent attacks on convoys crossing the Pakistan–Afghanistan border. See "Drivers Carrying NATO Supplies Through Pakistan Fear Attacks After Afghan Border Closed," Associated Press, November 26, 2011. See also Salman Masood and Eric Schmitt, "Tensions Flare Between U.S. and Pakistan After Strike," *New York Times*, November 26, 2011. Nevertheless, as the commander of U.S. Transportation Command told a congressional committee in February 2012, ground transit through Pakistan "remains the quickest and most cost-effective route" for supplies entering Afghanistan. See William Fraser, U.S. Air Force and commander of U.S. Transportation Command, statement before the U.S. Senate Committee on Armed Services on the state of the command, February 28, 2012a, p. 4.

agreements with NDN partners permit the reverse transit of U.S. materiel through their territories.[18] Despite the higher costs, the availability of the NDN makes the U.S.-led NATO mission less dependent on continued cooperation from Pakistan and thus gives Washington a freer hand to take positions that Islamabad might not like without the attendant fear of retaliation.

It could also be argued that Pakistani assistance remains critical to the elimination of al Qaeda in Afghanistan and Pakistan, which, after completing a policy review during his first three months in office, President Obama asserted is the United States' principal goal for the region.[19] However, although senior U.S. officials have acknowledged that Pakistani counterterrorism efforts have helped to degrade al Qaeda's leadership and capabilities,[20] Pakistan has not been a consistently reliable partner in counterterrorism operations. Although Islamabad has moved against groups that threaten its own security and that of its neighbors—namely, the TTP and al Qaeda—it has been much less willing to crack down on entities it sees as having strategic value, such as the Haqqani network and LeT. Both of these organizations are of direct concern to the United States. The Haqqani network has become increasingly aggressive in attacking coalition forces in Afghanistan. LeT, which many observers believe Pakistan continues to provide with logistical and financial support, has expanded its combat presence in Afghanistan and trained westerners to conduct attacks in their home countries; in addition, in the wake of LeT's assault on Mumbai in November 2008, U.S. policymakers and military commanders are concerned that a second such attack on India by LeT could provoke a conventional war—or even a nuclear conflict—between India and Pakistan.[21]

Islamabad has also been prepared to make its national security collaboration dependent on conditions that do not square with U.S. counterterrorism objectives. In April 2012, for instance, Islamabad issued a list of stringent demands for beginning the process of reopening NATO supply lines into Afghanistan—including an immediate end to drone strikes and other missions launched from Pakistani territory,[22] which U.S. military planners have long considered vital to disrupting terrorist networks operating in the FATA and protecting U.S. troops fighting in Afghanistan.[23]

---

[18] William Fraser, U.S. Air Force and commander of U.S. Transportation Command, statement before the U.S. Senate Committee on Armed Services for the hearing to receive testimony on U.S. Pacific Command and U.S. Transportation Command in review of the defense authorization request for fiscal year 2013 and the Future Years Defense Program, February 28, 2012b, p. 20.

[19] "[W]e have a clear and focused goal: to disrupt, dismantle and defeat al Qaeda in Pakistan and Afghanistan, and to prevent their return to either country in the future." See Barack Obama, president of the United States, remarks on a new strategy for Afghanistan and Pakistan, Washington, D.C., March 27, 2009.

[20] See "Brennan: Post-9/11, U.S. Has 'Right Balance' Between Civil Liberties, Security," *PBS Newshour*, September 7, 2011.

[21] Joby Warrick and Karen DeYoung, "CIA Helped India, Pakistan Share Secrets in Probe of Mumbai Siege," *Washington Post*, February 16, 2009.

[22] Salman Masood and Declan Walsh, "Pakistan Gives U.S. a List of Demands, Including an End to C.I.A. Drone Strikes," *New York Times*, April 12, 2012. Indeed, Pakistan did not guarantee that it would, in fact, reopen supply lines through its territory even if Washington did submit to its demands.

[23] When the U.S. government publicly acknowledged the conduct of lethal drone strikes against terrorist targets for the first time on April 30, 2012, senior White House counterterrorism adviser John O. Brennan called them an "essential" counterterrorism tool. See John O. Brennan, assistant to the president for homeland security and counterterrorism, "The Ethics and Efficacy of the President's Counterterrorism Strategy," remarks, Woodrow Wilson Center, Washington, D.C., April 30, 2012. Brennan did not state where drone strikes have taken place, referring only to attacks "beyond hot battlefields like Afghanistan."

Again, this stipulation is not as serious as it first seems. Although Islamabad's demand would certainly deprive Washington of crucial Pakistani bases from which to launch drone strikes, the U.S.–Afghanistan Strategic Partnership Agreement enabled alternative arrangements. Under the terms of this accord, Washington is able to use facilities on Afghan territory for the purposes of combating al Qaeda and its affiliates—including, presumably, carrying out unmanned airborne attacks against militants encamped in the FATA. Moreover, the agreement will allow the United States to continue undertaking unilateral counterterrorism operations from Afghanistan even after U.S. and NATO combat forces depart in 2014.

Implications for Other U.S. Interests

The ways in which the Indo–Pakistani rivalry in Afghanistan develops have the potential to affect other U.S. interests in the region. For example, Iran could exploit Delhi's reliance on Central Asian trade routes and pipelines that cross its territory to pressure India into ignoring international sanctions aimed at crippling Iran's oil-reliant economy.[24] Had India taken no action to reduce its purchases of Iranian oil, U.S. law would have required Washington to enact commercial, business, and trade restrictions on India—a move that would inevitably harm bilateral relations.[25] Eager to avoid such an outcome, however, Delhi cut its imports of Iranian oil by about 20 percent, and the United States granted India a waiver from potential sanctions in June 2012.[26] Delhi has even managed to gain some advantage from Iran's inability to find markets for its petroleum. In May 2012, for example, the government struck a deal with Tehran to continue purchasing its oil with rupees (presumably at a steep discount and with Washington's tacit approval), which Iran would then use—in what is effectively a bartering arrangement—to purchase Indian products.[27] In short, despite its growing energy requirements, Delhi has yet to be adversely affected by pressure from Tehran.

Islamabad could equally try to exploit the issue of oil as a means of gaining leverage over U.S. policy. It could, for example, threaten to undermine the current suite of U.S.-led sanctions against Iran by increasingly turning to Tehran for it energy imports. On the surface, it appears that Pakistan has already made moves in this direction, asserting that it will continue developing a new pipeline that would enable it to import 5 percent of its natural gas needs from Iran beginning in 2014.[28] Washington has made it clear that any such construction would violate anti-Iranian sanctions and draw a response, which could presumably endanger the $1 bil-

---

[24] U.S. Energy Information Administration, "India," Washington, D.C., Country Analysis Brief, November 21, 2011. Iran is the source of 11 percent of Indian oil imports, which potentially gives it some latitude to influence Delhi's policies.

[25] Andrew Quinn, "U.S. Keeps India Waiting on Iran Sanctions Waiver," Reuters, May 7, 2012.

[26] Timothy Gardner and Susan Cornwell, "U.S. Exempts India, Not China, from Iran Sanctions," Reuters, June 11, 2012; Brahma Chellaney, "Troubled US-India-Iran Triangle: India Has to Factor in Its Needs with the US," *Economic Times*, June 22, 2012.

[27] "Clinton Presses India to Cut Iran Oil Imports," Associated Press, May 7, 2012. Washington has presumably acquiesced to this arrangement, which minimizes the impact of sanctions on the Indian economy while posing little danger that Iran could use the non-convertible rupees it earns to advance its nuclear weapon program. See Debiprasad Nayak and Biman Mukherji, "Tehran Sets Trade Deals with India Amid Curbs," *Wall Street Journal*, May 9, 2012. See also Jim Yardley, "Indians Host Clinton While Also Wooing Iran," *New York Times*, May 8, 2012.

[28] Adam Schreck and Chris Brummitt, "Iran Looks to Boost Energy Ties to Nearby Pakistan," Associated Press, March 1, 2012. See also U.S. Energy Information Administration, "Pakistan: Country Analysis Brief," June 30, 2010a; and Haris

lion in dedicated U.S. aid that has been set aside to help develop and strengthen Pakistan's power sector.[29] This is not something that Islamabad would likely risk, and its announcement of intent to complete the gas pipeline probably has more to do with meeting its urgent energy requirements—which became evident in 2012 after widespread blackouts sparked antigovernment riots—than with any concerted attempt to influence U.S. policy decisions.

In addition, alienating Pakistan could drive Islamabad increasingly into the orbits of China and Iran, to the displeasure of both India and the United States. However, China is already one of Pakistan's closest trade and military partners, a relationship driven by a mutual desire to contain Indian military and economic might rather than by factors external to the region. Moreover, reductions in U.S. military aid—particularly the U.S. decision to suspend more than $800 million in defense assistance to Pakistan until Pakistani counterterrorism cooperation improves—are far more likely than a small Indian military deployment in Afghanistan to drive Pakistan to seek Chinese military equipment and training.[30]

Summary

Though India is an increasingly important U.S. ally on global issues, Washington's overwhelming emphasis on counterterrorism objectives and its resulting dependence on Pakistan have, to date, created a dynamic in which, according to former U.S. Ambassador to India Robert D. Blackwill, "India does not figure in an important way in U.S. calculations regarding Afghanistan."[31] As the U.S. military prepares to draw down, it is too late in the game to continue placating Islamabad by opposing greater involvement by Delhi; indeed, the blue-ribbon Council on Foreign Relations/Aspen Institute India study group asserted that "the United States should not allow Pakistan to exercise a de facto veto over the dimensions of Indian involvement in Afghanistan."[32] The best way to prevent Afghanistan from sliding into the abyss is to ensure that another power committed to countering Pakistan's destabilizing influence helps fill the security void created by the drawdown of U.S. troops. India fits that bill.

Anwar, "Pakistan Seeks Russia's Help to Finance Iran Gas Pipeline," Bloomberg, March 29, 2012. In April 2012, a Pakistani delegation traveled to Moscow to secure Russian financing for the pipeline.

[29] Schreck and Brummitt, 2012. For details on U.S. energy projects in Pakistan, see U.S. Agency for International Development, "Pakistan: Energy Program," September 2011b. See also U.S. Agency for International Development, "Energy in Pakistan," working paper, April 2011a.

[30] Farhan Bokhari, "With U.S. Military Aid Cut, Pakistan Eyes China," CBS News, July 10, 2011.

[31] Robert D. Blackwill, "The Future of US–India Relations," speech hosted by the Confederation of Indian Industries, New Delhi, May 5, 2009.

[32] Clary, 2011, p. 19.

CHAPTER SIX

Implications for India

Indians increasingly believe that Delhi's current approach to Afghanistan has yielded few, if any, strategic benefits[1] and that India has much to gain by increasing its involvement in Afghanistan. However, although Indian national security strategy calls for greater use of the military for power projection in the region, it is not at all clear whether Delhi would want to become more engaged in Afghanistan or assume the roles that the United States will relinquish. Such an effort would require large amounts of money and manpower, and it may inspire Islamabad—which would almost certainly view increasing Indian influence in Afghanistan as a strategic defeat—to strike back at India as a result.[2]

That said, Pakistan may turn to anti-Indian proxies anyway; as C. Christine Fair told a congressional panel in November 2011, "as India continues its rise, Pakistan's reliance upon Islamic militancy, the only tool that it has to change India's trajectory, will increase, not decrease."[3] If so, the prospect of Pakistani-backed attacks should not deter India from taking an increasingly active role in Afghanistan in pursuit of its broader strategic interests.

The key question, then, is whether Delhi views the potential advantages to be gained by expanding its presence in Afghanistan as outweighing the problems that might result. The prospect of an eventual U.S. troop withdrawal has already sparked heated commentary in India on how best to shape its future Afghan policy. Although some commentators recommend that India cut its losses and eliminate its own Afghan outreach before the security situation deteriorates further,[4] the overriding sense in India appears to be that the government has been too passive in promoting its interests in Afghanistan. The government's decision to fold when its opposition to negotiations with the Taliban was ignored at the January 2010 London Conference was seen as indicative of this timidity. Rather than push back, Delhi issued a post-conference statement that it would accept talks with members of the Taliban who renounce violence, give up terrorism, and abide by the Afghan constitution. Columnists and commentators criticized the government for being "defeatist" and for being unable or unwilling to leverage India's contributions to Afghan stability to advance its strategic interests.[5]

---

[1] For example, Pant, 2011.

[2] McChrystal, 2009, p. 2-11.

[3] Fair, 2011b, p. 43.

[4] See, for example, D. Suba Chandran, "Plan B for India in Afghanistan: Let Pakistan Remain Entrapped," *Tribune*, January 12, 2011.

[5] Aunohita Mojumdar, "India's Role in Afghanistan: Narrow Vision Returns Meagre Gains," *Times of India*, April 17, 2010. Quote is from Subhash Kapila, "Afghanistan: London Conference 2010 a Strategic Failure," South Asia Analysis Group, Paper 3643, February 2, 2010.

Certainly, many Indians realize that their country's great power ambitions will be severely undermined so long as Delhi fails to protect its vital interests in its own backyard. The common refrain is that, if India aspires to be a regional power, much less a global one, Delhi must demonstrate that it has the ability and the political will to project its influence and affect events in Afghanistan to its advantage. Although most agree that this needs to entail a minimum level of political and economic engagement, the question of greater Indian military involvement in Afghanistan—ranging from increasing security for diplomatic and development projects, to training Afghan security forces, to conducting military counterterrorism operations within Afghanistan—has generated far more discussion.

The least assertive approach is for Delhi to continue its existing political engagement, private investment, and development programs in Afghanistan. Even if such efforts fail to drive changes that dramatically advance India's strategic objectives, they do contribute to stability and economic growth in Afghanistan and promote Indian economic and commercial interests.

At the same time, Delhi might pursue backup options designed to mitigate the impact of a deteriorating security situation.[6] India could quietly reengage the NA by offering political support, economic assistance, and possibly small-scale military assistance and training. Such an effort would enable India to play its "northern card" by undermining the Taliban's efforts to extend its influence.[7] To buttress this strategy, adherents argue that India should launch a diplomatic effort to coordinate with Russia, Iran, Uzbekistan, and Tajikistan—all of which share India's hostility to a resurgent Taliban—as well as open channels of communication with those elements of the Taliban that are most likely to resist Pakistani demands to train anti-India extremists in Afghanistan.[8]

A more direct policy would involve the deployment of additional security forces to protect India's diplomatic and economic presence in Afghanistan. Soon after the first bombing of Delhi's embassy in Kabul, the *Indian Express* voiced support for such an approach in an editorial column, writing,

> After the Kabul bombing, India must come to terms with an important question that it has avoided debating so far. New Delhi cannot continue to expand its economic and diplomatic activity in Afghanistan, while avoiding a commensurate increase in its military presence there. . . . If withdrawal is not an option, India must quickly find ways to minimize the risk to its diplomats.[9]

Under this scenario, security missions would remain entirely defensive in nature and would not go beyond the protection of Indian government personnel, facilities, and investments. Security forces could be charged with safeguarding Indian citizens and facilities related to private-sector projects, as well as to government initiatives, but, otherwise, the mission would simply be an expansion of the existing Indian deployment.

A third and yet more assertive policy would be for Delhi to continue providing training to Afghan security forces in India. Although Indian military assistance would not approach

---

[6] S. Chandra, 2011, pp. 125–127.

[7] S. Chandra, 2011.

[8] Tadjbakhsh, 2011, p. 45; S. Chandra, 2011, pp. 125–127. See also Sharma, 2009, p. 3.

[9] "After Kabul," *Indian Express*, July 8, 2008, as quoted in Iftikhar A. Lodhi, "Attack on the Indian Embassy in Kabul: Time to Sober Up," Singapore: Institute of South Asian Studies, Brief 75, July 15, 2008.

the scale of that provided by the United States in the past decade, it would advance similar objectives: building a professional Afghan army that can project the central government's power throughout the country while also developing Afghan counterterrorism capabilities so as to eliminate the safe havens used by anti-India extremists.[10]

The October 2011 Indo-Afghan Strategic Partnership Agreement has already moved Delhi in this direction by committing the government to train small numbers of Afghan security personnel in counterterrorism and COIN tactics.[11] All training called for by the agreement would take place in India, however, thus avoiding the provocative—and controversial—step of sending Indian troops to Afghanistan itself.

A fourth approach would be to expand the types and extent of training being provided to Afghan military and police beyond what was agreed to in the strategic partnership agreement. A blue-ribbon panel convened by the Council on Foreign Relations and the Aspen Institute India recommended that the United States and Delhi consider whether large-scale military training would be productive, though it also cautioned that "such discussions should include consideration of possible counterproductive Pakistani reaction before deciding on any course of action."[12]

If Delhi decided to be even more forceful, a fifth option would be to conduct security training inside Afghanistan. Although this would enable small teams of Indian instructors to engage many more Afghans, the presence of even limited numbers of Indian forces on Afghan territory would make officials in Islamabad nervous, to say the least, and increase Indo-Pakistani tensions.

The sixth and most aggressive strategy would entail deploying Indian forces to train their Afghan counterparts inside Afghanistan *and* to conduct anti-Taliban counterterrorism and COIN operations alongside them. Delhi's use of this type of "hard power" would take the fight to the militants, so to speak, through proactive, preventive action. As Sushant K. Singh, editor of the Indian journal *Pragati*, observes,

> An Indian military involvement in Afghanistan will shift the battleground away from Kashmir and the Indian mainland. Targeting the jihadi base will be a huge boost for India's anti-terrorist operations, especially in Kashmir, both militarily and psychologically.[13]

---

[10] India's own counterterrorism capabilities are less than perfect, as demonstrated by its security forces' performance during the Mumbai attack and its difficulty in combating Naxalites throughout central, southern, and eastern states and insurgents in northeastern India. Nevertheless, India has made improvements to its counterterrorism capabilities as a direct result of the lessons learned from the Mumbai attacks, and Indian security forces could certainly offer effective training to their less professional and less competent Afghan counterparts.

[11] Bassam Javed, "Indian Role in Afghanistan Spells Danger for Pakistan," *International News*, February 10, 2012; "India Decides to Train Afghanistan's Army and Signs Other Bilateral Agreements with Afghanistan," 2011. See also Ganguly, 2011; and "Indo-Afghan Strategic Partnership," 2011.

[12] Clary, 2011, p. 19.

[13] Singh, 2008, pp. 12–13.

An in-country presence of this sort would also enable India to provide security along the northern trade routes to the CARs.[14] Rather than waiting until 2014, India could conceivably embark upon this strategy even while U.S. and NATO forces remain in Afghanistan.[15]

An Indian combat deployment to Afghanistan, however, is extremely unlikely. An Indian military deployment would undermine the considerable goodwill that India has cultivated in Afghanistan by making it appear as if Delhi is intervening to advance the interests of its historical Tajik and Uzbek partners, to the detriment of ethnic Pashtuns. Furthermore, the specter of India's disastrous military intervention in Sri Lanka from 1987 to 1990—which cost the lives of 1,500 Indian soldiers and contributed to the Tamil Tigers' assassination of India's Prime Minister Rajiv Gandhi in 1991[16]—would likely dissuade Indian decisionmakers from becoming entangled in another low-intensity conflict that poses only indirect threats to Indian security. Perhaps with this experience in mind, Indian External Affairs Minister S. M. Krishna stated, during an Indian television interview in October 2011, "India doesn't believe in the concept of sending troops to any country except at a time under United Nations auspices for peacekeeping purposes."[17]

Most importantly, Islamabad would see any Indian military presence in Afghanistan as extremely provocative and would, as General McChrystal predicted, respond aggressively. An Indian deployment would undermine the Pakistani military's confidence that it could use Afghan territory for the strategic depth that it believes is militarily necessary. Even India's soft-power initiatives created a perception among Pakistan's military elites that "India was taking over Afghanistan," as scholar Harsh Pant writes, thereby propelling "Pakistan's security establishment into panic mode."[18] Senior Pakistani officials have already expressed disapproval of Delhi's offer to provide military training to Afghan security forces, no matter whether it is conducted inside Afghanistan or elsewhere. As Pakistani Army Chief of Staff General Ashfaq Parvez Kayani asserted, "Strategically, we cannot have an Afghan army on our western border which has an Indian mindset and capabilities to take on Pakistan."[19] Given this reaction, it seems clear that Indian troops engaging in extensive military training—not to mention military operations—inside Afghanistan would be a bridge too far for the Pakistani military.

Pakistan's retaliatory options, however, offer little immediate benefit to the country and could even undermine its own interests. Islamabad could block Afghan exports to India, although such a step would harm Kabul far more than it would Delhi and thus potentially engender anti-Pakistani sentiment in Afghanistan. It could pull out of the TAPI pipeline deal, but Pakistan needs to import energy resources from Central Asia as much as India does, if not more. In place of TAPI, Pakistan could construct a multi-billion-dollar pipeline to import gas from neighboring Iran—for which it is seeking Chinese and Russian funding—but tightening

---

[14] Singh, 2008, p. 12.

[15] Nitin Pai and Rohit Pradhan, "Why India Must Send Troops to Afghanistan," *Pragati: The Indian National Interest Review*, January 1, 2010.

[16] International Crisis Group, *India and Sri Lanka After the LTTE*, Washington, D.C., Asia Report 206, June 23, 2011, p. 3.

[17] Suhasini Haidar, "10 Years Later: Is India the US' Next Option in Afghanistan?" IBN Live, October 12, 2011.

[18] Pant, 2011, p. 33.

[19] Sahgal, 2011, p. 116.

international sanctions on Iran make such a move impractical.[20] It could seek greater assistance from China, but Beijing already supports Pakistan on a range of initiatives designed to advance their mutual objective of containing Indian influence, including investing in the port at Gwadar and selling Chinese military materiel to the Pakistani army.

Islamabad could, as noted, retaliate against Delhi by escalating insurgent activity in Kashmir or encouraging additional Mumbai-style terrorist strikes. However, given the long history of attacks on India by Pakistani-backed extremists, it is doubtful that the Indian population would immediately associate a future act of political violence in the country with Delhi's expeditionary activities in Afghanistan. Even if such a link was made, it is questionable that the public would hold its own government accountable for "provoking" an attack by pursuing its Afghan interests—just as Americans (with a few vocal exceptions) refused to accept the al Qaeda narrative that the U.S. government incited the 9/11 attacks through its policies toward the Muslim world.

Despite Pakistan's limited options for effective direct retaliation, India is unlikely to risk undermining the strategic benefits of a more proactive regional approach by provocatively deploying combat troops or trainers to Afghanistan. Delhi's more likely course of action, therefore, would be to institute moderately more assertive measures while also developing backup options to hedge its bets in the bilateral relationship with Kabul. Although India may opt to deploy additional paramilitary forces (such as the ITBP) to protect Indian diplomats and aid workers, and although it might seek to expand military instruction beyond the minimal levels called for in the Indo-Afghan Strategic Partnership Agreement, Delhi is unlikely to engage in large-scale training missions or pursue concerted counterterrorism or COIN operations directly on Afghan soil.

India will probably keep its political options open as well. For example, while continuing to support the Karzai government, the Indian government will quietly attempt to build contacts with Taliban figures who participate in the reconciliation process to prevent them from treating India with hostility if they secure roles in a future Afghan government. Delhi may also decide to resume a measure of support to its erstwhile NA partners just in case a future regime in Kabul—particularly one in which Pakistani-controlled Taliban play leading roles—turns out to be less than friendly. Furthermore, while continuing to highlight to U.S. policymakers the general congruence of U.S. and Indian policies vis-à-vis Afghanistan, India can also be expected to engage Russia, Iran, Tajikistan, and Uzbekistan in collaborative efforts to prevent a potential return of the Taliban. Finally, if it is not already doing so, Delhi might begin building an infrastructure to support Baloch separatists operating in Pakistan as a contingency for responding (in a non-attributable manner) to ISI-sponsored jihadi attacks against Indian interests and territory.

---

[20] See "Pak Assures Iran on Gas Pipeline Project," Press Trust of India, February 16, 2012; Syed Fazl-e-Haider, "Pakistan Defiant on Iran Gas Pipeline," *Asia Times*, February 9, 2012; and Zeeshan Javaid, "Russia Agrees to Finance IP Gas Pipeline Project," *Daily Times*, June 28, 2012.

CHAPTER SEVEN

Conclusion

Currently, India and Pakistan have very different visions of what Afghanistan should look like, and they seek to advance highly disparate interests through their respective strategies for engaging the country. Islamabad views Afghanistan primarily as an environment in which to pursue its rivalry with India. To this end, Pakistan seeks a significant role for the Taliban in a generally weak Kabul government so as to extend its own influence in the country, minimize that of Delhi, and preserve its use of Afghan territory as a training ground for militant proxy groups that Islamabad sees as strategic assets in its ongoing conflict with India. Secondary goals include using Afghanistan as a conduit to the energy-rich CARs, which has been complicated by Pakistan's past support of Central Asian Islamist groups; isolating Afghanistan by preventing it from integrating into the South and Central Asian regional economy; and forging closer relations with Russia and Iran.

By contrast, India pursues interests that require Afghanistan to experience stability and economic growth—notably, protecting itself from terrorism, expanding commerce, securing Central Asian energy resources, and establishing itself as a regional power. Thus, whereas Pakistan seeks to fashion an Afghan state that would detract from regional security, India's objectives for Afghanistan would enhance Afghanistan's political stability, security, economic growth, reconstruction, and regional integration.

In the short term, Kabul would likely welcome some degree of increased Indian involvement in its reconstruction and security. However, given President Karzai's perpetual need to balance the interests of superior competing forces, it is entirely possible that he will welcome Indian assistance and then take subsequent steps to accommodate Pakistan in ways that at least partially negate what India had achieved. Furthermore, should a government emerge in Kabul that is dominated by the Taliban or strongly influenced by Islamabad, it would almost certainly seek to reverse its relations with Delhi. This necessarily means that an integral component of any Indian effort to increase its involvement in Afghanistan must include a willingness to maintain commitments in a post-Karzai (as well as a post-NATO) environment.

Not only does Delhi have more to offer the broader South and Central Asian regions than Islamabad; Indian assistance to Afghan security forces, combined with an increasingly proactive Indian role in Afghanistan's economic and commercial development, offers the best hope for entrenching—and even advancing—U.S. achievements in that part of the world. In Afghanistan, Delhi is in a position to promote political stability, boost trade, foster development, contribute to security-sector capacity-building, and—perhaps most significantly of all—counter the terrorist groups that directly threaten the vital interests of both India and the United States. In helping bring greater stability to Afghanistan, India would thus increase its own physical and economic security while preserving and furthering Washington's own contributions to Afghanistan's reconstruction. As the United States prepares to draw down its combat forces from Afghanistan in 2014, it should therefore encourage India to fill the potential security vacuum by adopting an increasingly assertive political, economic, and security strategy that includes the provision of additional military training and possibly the deployment of Indian troops.

References

Abshire, David M., and Ryan Browne, "The Missing Endgame for Afghanistan: A Sustainable Post–bin Laden Strategy," *Washington Quarterly*, Vol. 34, No. 4, Fall 2011, pp. 59–72. As of June 18, 2012:
http://csis.org/publication/twq-missing-endgame-afghanistan-sustainable-post-bin-laden-strategy

"Afghanistan Wants Indian Investments: Singh," *Daily Outlook Afghanistan*, November 14, 2011. As of June 15, 2012:
http://www.outlookafghanistan.net/news?post_id=2511

"Afghans Mourn After Killing of Peace Negotiator," Associated Press, May 14, 2012.

"After Kabul," *Indian Express*, July 8, 2008. As of June 19, 2012:
http://www.indianexpress.com/news/after-kabul/332675/0

Agreement Between the Governments of the Islamic Republic of Afghanistan and the Islamic Republic of Pakistan: Afghanistan–Pakistan Transit Trade Agreement, 2010 (APTTA), October 28, 2010. As of June 18, 2012:
http://www.commerce.gov.pk/APTTA/APTTA.pdf

Ahmad, Sardar, "28 Killed in Suicide Attack at India's Afghanistan Embassy," Agence France-Presse, July 7, 2008.

Alexander, Chris, "Afghanistan and Pakistan: A Strategy for Peace," *Options Politiques*, November 2010, pp. 30–35. As of June 18, 2012:
http://www.irpp.org/po/archive/nov10/alexander.pdf

Allbritton, Chris, "Holbrooke Hails Pakistan–U.S. Collaboration on Taliban," Reuters, February 18, 2010. As of June 18, 2012:
http://www.reuters.com/article/2010/02/18/us-pakistan-taliban-idUSTRE61H2QO20100218

Anand, Vinod, "Pakistan as a Factor in Afghan Stability," in R. K. Sawhney, Arun Sahgal, and Gurmeet Kanwal, eds., *Afghanistan: A Role for India*, New Delhi: Centre for Land Warfare Studies, 2011, pp. 141–162.

Aneja, Atul, "India and Afghanistan: The Way Forward," *The Hindu*, January 4, 2011. As of June 15, 2012:
http://www.hindu.com/2011/01/04/stories/2011010451521200.htm

Anwar, Haris, "Pakistan Seeks Russia's Help to Finance Iran Gas Pipeline," Bloomberg, March 29, 2012. As of June 19, 2012:
http://www.bloomberg.com/news/2012-03-29/
pakistan-sending-team-to-russia-to-seek-iran-gas-pipeline-help.html

Arnoldy, Ben, "How the Afghanistan War Became Tangled in India vs. Pakistan Rivalry," *Christian Science Monitor*, January 20, 2011. As of June 28, 2012:
http://www.csmonitor.com/World/Asia-South-Central/2011/0120/
How-the-Afghanistan-war-became-tangled-in-India-vs.-Pakistan-rivalry

"Asim Hussain Paints a Dire Picture of the Gas Crisis," *Express Tribune*, January 3, 2012.

Baabar, Mariana, "Pakistan to Train Afghan Troops," *International News*, November 4, 2011. As of June 18, 2012:
http://www.thenews.com.pk/TodaysPrintDetail.aspx?ID=10067&Cat=13

Bajoria, Jayshree, "India-Afghanistan Relations," Council on Foreign Relations backgrounder, July 22, 2009. As of June 15, 2012:
http://www.cfr.org/india/india-afghanistan-relations/p17474

Barfield, Thomas J., *Afghanistan: A Cultural and Political History*, Princeton, N.J.: Princeton University Press, 2010.

Bentley, John, "Leon Panetta: U.S. 'Reaching the Limits of Our Patience' with Pakistan Terror Safe Havens," CBS News, June 7, 2012. As of July 17, 2012:
http://www.cbsnews.com/8301-503543_162-57448784-503543/
leon-panetta-u.s--reaching-the-limits-of-our-patience-with-pakistan-terror-safe-havens/

Bhasin, Avtar Singh, ed., *India's Foreign Relations, 2007: Part I*, New Delhi: Ministry of External Affairs and Geetika Publishers, 2008.

———, ed., *India's Foreign Relations, 2008: Part I*, New Delhi: Ministry of External Affairs and Geetika Publishers, 2009.

"Biography," Office of the President, Islamic Republic of Afghanistan, undated. As of June 15, 2012:
http://president.gov.af/en/Page/1043

Blackwill, Robert D., "The Future of US–India Relations," speech hosted by the Confederation of Indian Industries, New Delhi, May 5, 2009. As of June 19, 2012:
http://www.aspenindia.org/outreach/pdf/Blackwill_speech_May_05_2009.pdf

Blair, Dennis, Director of National Intelligence, *Annual Threat Assessment of the US Intelligence Community for the Senate Select Committee on Intelligence*, February 2, 2010. As of June 18, 2012:
http://www.dni.gov/testimonies/20100202_testimony.pdf

Blake, Robert O. Jr., assistant secretary, Bureau of South and Central Asian Affairs, U.S. Department of State, "The Obama Administration's Priorities in South and Central Asia," remarks, Houston, Texas, January 19, 2011a. As of June 15, 2012:
http://www.state.gov/p/sca/rls/rmks/2011/155002.htm

———, testimony before the U.S. House of Representatives Committee on Foreign Affairs, Subcommittee on the Middle East and South Asia, April 5, 2011b. As of June 18, 2012:
http://foreignaffairs.house.gov/112/65627.pdf

———, "Looking Ahead: U.S.–India Strategic Relations and the Transpacific Century," remarks, National Bureau of Asian Research, Washington, D.C., September 28, 2011c. As of June 18, 2012:
http://www.state.gov/p/sca/rls/rmks/2011/174139.htm

Blanchard, Christopher M., *Afghanistan: Narcotics and U.S. Policy*, Washington, D.C.: Congressional Research Service, RL32686, August 12, 2009.

Bodansky, Yossef, *Islamabad's Road Warriors*, Houston, Texas: Freeman Center for Strategic Studies, 1995.

Bokhari, Farhan, "With U.S. Military Aid Cut, Pakistan Eyes China," CBS News, July 10, 2011. As of June 19, 2012:
http://www.cbsnews.com/8301-503543_162-20078219-503543.html

Brennan, John O., assistant to the president for homeland security and counterterrorism, "The Ethics and Efficacy of the President's Counterterrorism Strategy," remarks, Woodrow Wilson Center, Washington, D.C., April 30, 2012. As of June 19, 2012:
http://www.wilsoncenter.org/event/the-efficacy-and-ethics-us-counterterrorism-strategy

"Brennan: Post-9/11, U.S. Has 'Right Balance' Between Civil Liberties, Security," *PBS Newshour*, September 7, 2011. As of June 19, 2012:
http://www.pbs.org/newshour/bb/politics/july-dec11/johnbrennan_09-07.html

Brummitt, Chris, "NATO Invites Pakistan to Summit in Chicago," Associated Press, May 15, 2012.

Bumiller, Elisabeth, and Jane Perlez, "Pakistan's Spies Linked to Raid on US Embassy," *Boston Globe*, September 23, 2011. As of June 18, 2012:
http://www.bostonglobe.com/news/world/2011/09/22/pakistan-aided-embassy-strike-mullen-says/
ysOg2WMdqrO1Ge4jvm5mZJ/story.html

Bush, George W., *The National Security Strategy*, Washington, D.C.: White House, March 2006. As of June 19, 2012:
http://georgewbush-whitehouse.archives.gov/nsc/nss/2006/

Chandra, Satish, "India's Options in Afghanistan," *Strategic Analysis*, Vol. 35, No. 1, January 2011, pp. 125–127.

Chandra, Vishal, "The Afghan Maze and India's Options," seminar, New Delhi: Institute for Defence Studies and Analyses, September 4, 2009. As of June 14, 2012:
http://www.idsa.in/?q=event/TheAfghanMazeandIndiasOptions_vchandra_04092009

Chandran, D. Suba, "Plan B for India in Afghanistan: Let Pakistan Remain Entrapped," *Tribune*, January 12, 2011. As of June 19, 2012:
http://www.tribuneindia.com/2011/20110112/edit.htm#4

Chaudet, Didier, "Islamist Terrorism in Greater Central Asia: The 'al-Qaedaization' of Uzbek Jihadism," *Russia.Nie.Visions*, No. 35, December 2008. As of June 18, 2012:
http://www.ifri.org/?page=contribution-detail&id=5211&id_provenance=97

Chaudhry, Sajid, "$7.6 Billion TAPI Gas Pipeline Project," *Daily Times*, November 13, 2011. As of June 14, 2012:
http://www.dailytimes.com.pk/default.asp?page=2011%5C11%5C13%5Cstory_13-11-2011_pg7_20

Chellaney, Brahma, "Troubled US-India-Iran Triangle: India Has to Factor in Its Needs with the US," *Economic Times*, June 22, 2012. As of June 25, 2012:
http://articles.economictimes.indiatimes.com/2012-06-22/news/32369070_1_india-and-iran-iran-sanctions-act-purchases-of-iranian-oil

Clary, Christopher, *The United States and India: A Shared Strategic Future*, New York: Council on Foreign Relations Press, 2011.

Clinton, Hillary, Secretary of State, "Certification Relating to Pakistan Under Section 203 of the Enhanced Partnership with Pakistan Act of 2009 (P.L. 111-73)," March 18, 2011, in Jacquelyn L. Williams-Bridgers, *Pakistan Assistance: Relatively Little of the $3 Billion in Requested Assistance Is Subject to State's Certification of Pakistan's Progress on Nonproliferation and Counterterrorism Issues*, Washington, D.C.: U.S. Government Accountability Office, GAO-11-786R, July 19, 2011a, p. 10. As of June 14, 2012:
http://purl.fdlp.gov/GPO/gpo12097

———, "Remarks at the New Silk Road Ministerial Meeting," New York, September 22, 2011b. As of June 18, 2012:
http://www.state.gov/secretary/rm/2011/09/173807.htm

"Clinton Presses India to Cut Iran Oil Imports," Associated Press, May 7, 2012.

Cloud, David S., and Alex Rodriguez, "CIA Gets Nod to Step Up Drone Strikes in Pakistan," *Los Angeles Times*, June 8, 2012. As of June 25, 2012:
http://articles.latimes.com/2012/jun/08/world/la-fg-pakistan-drone-surge-20120608

Cloughley, Brian, "Uneasy Partnership: The US and Pakistan's Dysfunctional Alliance," *Jane's Intelligence Review*, April 14, 2010.

"Clueless in Afghanistan," *LiveMint*, January 27, 2010. As of June 14, 2012:
http://www.livemint.com/2010/01/27202745/Clueless-in-Afghanistan.html

Coll, Steve, "War by Other Means," *New Yorker*, May 24, 2010.

Combined Maritime Forces, undated web page. As of June 14, 2012:
http://www.cusnc.navy.mil/cmf/cmf_command.html

DeYoung, Karen, "Pakistan Border Closure Costs U.S. $100 Million a Month," *Washington Post*, June 13, 2012. As of June 25, 2012:
http://www.washingtonpost.com/world/national-security/pakistan-border-closure-costs-us-100-million-a-month/2012/06/13/gJQAqhCfaV_story.html

Dreyfuss, Robert, "Like It or Not, America Needs Pakistan," *Inquirer,* November 30, 2011. As of June 19, 2012:
http://articles.philly.com/2011-11-30/
news/30459108_1_pakistani-government-pakistani-officials-pakistani-soldiers

"Drivers Carrying NATO Supplies Through Pakistan Fear Attacks After Afghan Border Closed," Associated Press, November 26, 2011.

D'Souza, Shanthie Mariet, "Hold Steady in Afghanistan," *Pragati: The Indian National Interest Review,* No. 17, August 2008, pp. 9–11. As of June 15, 2012:
http://pragati.nationalinterest.in/wp-content/uploads/2008/08/pragati-issue17-aug2008-communityed.pdf

———, *India, Afghanistan and the 'End Game'?* Singapore: Institute of South Asian Studies, Working Paper 124, March 24, 2011.

Dwyer, Devin, "Osama Bin Laden Killing: Pakistan Reacts Cautiously to U.S. Raid on Its Soil," ABC News, May 2, 2011. As of June 14, 2012:
http://abcnews.go.com/Politics/osama-bin-laden-killed-pakistan-reacts-cautiously-us/
story?id=13507918#.T9o5PytYv7g

Enduring Strategic Partnership Agreement Between the United States of America and the Islamic Republic of Afghanistan, Kabul, May 24, 2012. As of June 14, 2012:
http://www.whitehouse.gov/sites/default/files/2012.06.01u.s.-afghanistanspasignedtext.pdf

External Publicity Division, Ministry of External Affairs, Government of India, *India and Afghanistan: A Development Partnership,* c. 2009. As of June 15, 2012:
http://www.mea.gov.in/staticfile/report.pdf

Faiez, M. Karim, and Mark Magnier, "Taliban Claims Responsibility for Kabul Embassy Attack," *Los Angeles Times,* October 9, 2009. As of June 18, 2012:
http://articles.latimes.com/2009/oct/09/world/fg-afghanistan-bomb9

Fair, C. Christine, *India in Afghanistan and Beyond: Opportunities and Constraints,* Washington, D.C.: Century Foundation, 2010a. As of June 15, 2012:
http://tcf.org/publications/2010/9/india-in-afghanistan-and-beyond-opportunities-and-constraints/pdf

———, "India in Afghanistan, Part I: Strategic Interests, Regional Concerns," *Foreign Policy,* October 26, 2010b. As of June 15, 2012:
http://afpak.foreignpolicy.com/posts/2010/10/26/
india_in_afghanistan_part_1_strategic_interests_regional_concerns

———, "Under the Shrinking U.S. Security Umbrella: India's End Game in Afghanistan?" *Washington Quarterly,* Vol. 34, No. 2, Spring 2011a, pp. 179–192. As of June 15, 2012:
http://csis.org/publication/twq-under-shrinking-us-security-umbrella-indias-end-game-afghanistan

———, "2014 and Beyond: U.S. Policy Towards Afghanistan and Pakistan, Part I," testimony before the U.S. House of Representatives Committee on Foreign Affairs Subcommittee on the Middle East and South Asia, November 3, 2011b. As of June 14, 2012:
http://foreignaffairs.house.gov/112/71039.pdf

Fair, C. Christine, and Peter Chalk, *Fortifying Pakistan: The Role of US Internal Security Assistance,* Washington, D.C.: U.S. Institute of Peace, 2006.

Farmer, Ben, "Suicide Bombers Target Kabul Hotels Killing Seventeen," *Telegraph,* February 26, 2010. As of June 18, 2012:
http://www.telegraph.co.uk/news/worldnews/asia/afghanistan/7325937/
Suicide-bombers-target-Kabul-hotels-killing-seventeen.html

———, "Hamid Karzai Says He Will Not Seek Third Term," *Telegraph,* August 11, 2011. As of June 18, 2012:
http://www.telegraph.co.uk/news/worldnews/asia/afghanistan/8695924/
Hamid-Karzai-says-he-will-not-seek-third-term.html

Fazl-e-Haider, Syed, "Pakistan Defiant on Iran Gas Pipeline," *Asia Times*, February 9, 2012. As of June 19, 2012:
http://www.atimes.com/atimes/South_Asia/NB09Df02.html

Feldman, Daniel F., deputy special representative for Afghanistan and Pakistan, U.S. Department of State, testimony before the U.S. House of Representatives Committee on Foreign Affairs, Subcommittee on the Middle East and South Asia, April 5, 2011. As of June 18, 2012:
http://foreignaffairs.house.gov/112/65627.pdf

Fifield, Anna, "Pakistan Lets China See US Helicopter," *Financial Times*, August 14, 2011.

Fraser, William, U.S. Air Force and commander of U.S. Transportation Command, statement before the U.S. Senate Committee on Armed Services on the state of the command, February 28, 2012a. As of June 19, 2012:
http://armed-services.senate.gov/statemnt/2012/02%20February/Fraser%2002-28-12.pdf

———, statement before the U.S. Senate Committee on Armed Services for the hearing to receive testimony on U.S. Pacific Command and U.S. Transportation Command in review of the defense authorization request for fiscal year 2013 and the Future Years Defense Program, February 28, 2012b. As of June 19, 2012:
http://armed-services.senate.gov/Transcripts/2012/02%20February/12-04%20-%202-28-12.pdf

Ganguly, Sumit, "India and the Afghan Endgame," *Diplomat*, November 14, 2011. As of June 15, 2012:
http://thediplomat.com/indian-decade/2011/11/14/india-and-the-afghan-endgame/

Ganguly, Sumit, and Nicholas Howenstein, "India–Pakistan Rivalry in Afghanistan," *Journal of International Affairs*, Vol. 63, No. 1, Fall–Winter 2009, pp. 127–140.

Gannon, Kathy, "Vengeful New Militant Group Emerges in Pakistan," Associated Press, July 1, 2010.

Garamone, Jim, "U.S. Reaching Limit of Patience with Pakistan on Safe Havens," American Forces Press Service, June 7, 2012. As of June 25, 2012:
http://www.defense.gov/news/newsarticle.aspx?id=116656

Gardner, Timothy, and Susan Cornwell, "U.S. Exempts India, Not China, from Iran Sanctions," Reuters, June 11, 2012.

Goldberg, Jeffrey, and Marc Ambinder, "The Ally from Hell," *Atlantic*, December 2011. As of June 14, 2012:
http://www.theatlantic.com/magazine/archive/2011/12/the-ally-from-hell/8730/#

Grare, Frédéric, "Pakistan," in Ashley J. Tellis and Aroop Mukharji, eds., *Is a Regional Strategy Viable in Afghanistan?* Washington, D.C.: Carnegie Endowment for International Peace, 2010, pp. 17–26. As of June 14, 2012:
http://www.carnegieendowment.org/files/regional_approach.pdf

Gul, Imtiaz, "Pakistan's New Networks of Terror," *Foreign Policy*, June 10, 2010. As of June 18, 2012:
http://www.foreignpolicy.com/articles/2010/06/10/pakistans_new_networks_of_terror

Gundu, Raja Karthikeya, and Teresita C. Schaffer, "India and Pakistan in Afghanistan: Hostile Sports," *South Asia Monitor*, No. 117, April 3, 2008. As of June 15, 2012:
http://csis.org/publication/south-asia-monitor-india-and-pakistan-afghanistan-hostile-sports-april-03-2008

"Gunmen Kill Senior Afghan Peace Negotiator," MSNBC, May 13, 2012. As of June 18, 2012:
http://worldnews.msnbc.msn.com/_news/2012/05/13/
11682161-gunmen-kill-senior-afghan-peace-negotiator?lite

Haidar, Suhasini, "10 Years Later: Is India the US' Next Option in Afghanistan?" IBN Live, October 12, 2011. As of July 23, 2012:
http://ibnlive.in.com/videos/192437/10-yrs-in-afghanistan-should-the-us-pull-out-its-troops.html

Harrison, Selig S., "Afghanistan's Tyranny of the Minority," *New York Times*, August 16, 2009. As of June 18, 2012:
http://www.nytimes.com/2009/08/17/opinion/17harrison.html

Haté, Vibhuti, "India's Energy Dilemma," *South Asia Monitor*, No. 98, September 7, 2006. As of June 14, 2012:
http://csis.org/files/media/csis/pubs/sam98.pdf

Hirsh, Michael, "Pakistan: The Terror State We Call Our Ally," *Atlantic*, May 25, 2012. As of June 14, 2012:
http://www.theatlantic.com/international/archive/2012/05/pakistan-the-terror-state-we-call-our-ally/257699/

Hodge, Nathan, "U.S. Secures New Afghan Exit Routes," *Wall Street Journal*, February 29, 2012.

Hussain, Ijaz, "Implications of SAARC Enlargement," *Daily Times*, November 23, 2005. As of June 18, 2012:
http://www.dailytimes.com.pk/default.asp?page=2005%5C11%5C23%5Cstory_23-11-2005_pg3_5

"In a Sulk: Relations Grow Yet Worse Between Pakistan and the Superpower," *Economist*, July 14, 2011. As of June 18, 2012:
http://www.economist.com/node/18959707

"India," *World Factbook*, Washington, D.C.: Central Intelligence Agency, updated November 8, 2011. As of June 14, 2012:
https://www.cia.gov/library/publications/the-world-factbook/geos/in.html

"India: Afghanistan's Influential Ally," BBC News, October 8, 2009. As of June 15, 2012:
http://news.bbc.co.uk/2/hi/south_asia/7492982.stm

"India and United Nations: Peacekeeping and Peacebuilding," United Nations, undated. As of June 14, 2012:
http://www.un.int/india/india_and_the_un_pkeeping.html

"India Decides to Train Afghanistan's Army and Signs Other Bilateral Agreements with Afghanistan," *Defence Now*, October 7, 2011. As of June 15, 2012:
http://www.defencenow.com/news/322/
india-decides-to-train-afghanistans-army-and-signs-other-bilateral-agreements-with-afghanistan.html

"India Green Lights Military Assistance to Nepal," *Himalayan*, January 18, 2012. As of June 14, 2012:
http://www.thehimalayantimes.com/
fullNews.php?headline=India+green+lights+military+assistance+to+Nepal++&NewsID=317173

"Indian Car Market Growth Second Fastest Globally," *Times of India*, January 12, 2011. As of June 14, 2012:
http://articles.timesofindia.indiatimes.com/2011-01-12/
india-business/28352452_1_global-auto-commercial-vehicles-indian-automobile-manufacturers

"India's Role in Afghanistan," *IISS Strategic Comments*, Vol. 17, June 2011.

"India to Cut Tariff on Imported Goods from Afghanistan," *TOLOnews*, June 6, 2011. As of June 18, 2012:
http://tolonews.com/index.php?option=com_content&view=article&id=2922:
india-to-cut-tariff-on-imported-goods-from-afghanistan&catid=3:business&Itemid=99&lang=en

"India to Train Kyrgyz Armed Forces, Establish Military Ties in Central Asia," *Defence Now*, July 19, 2011. As of June 14, 2012:
http://www.defencenow.com/news/246/
india-to-train-kyrgyz-armed-forces-establish-military-ties-in-central-asia.html

"Indo-Afghan Commercial Relations," Embassy of India in Kabul, undated. As of June 15, 2012:
http://meakabul.nic.in/pdfs/commercialrelations.pdf

"Indo-Afghan Strategic Partnership," *Daily Times*, October 6, 2011. As of June 15, 2012:
http://www.dailytimes.com.pk/default.asp?page=2011%5C10%5C06%5Cstory_6-10-2011_pg3_1

International Crisis Group, *India and Sri Lanka After the LTTE*, Washington, D.C., Asia Report 206, June 23, 2011. As of June 19, 2012:
http://www.crisisgroup.org/~/media/Files/asia/south-asia/sri-lanka/
206%20India%20and%20Sri%20Lanka%20after%20the%20LTTE.pdf

Jacob, Jayanth, "India Shuffles Its Northern Card," *Hindustan Times*, August 9, 2010. As of June 15, 2012:
http://www.hindustantimes.com/India-news/NewDelhi/India-shuffles-its-Northern-card/
Article1-584429.aspx

Jacob, Jayanth, and Saubhadra Chatterji, "India's Track 3: Afghan–Iran Rail Link," *Hindustan Times*, November 1, 2011. As of June 18, 2012:
http://www.hindustantimes.com/India-news/NewDelhi/India-s-Track-3-Afghan-Iran-rail-link/
Article1-763448.aspx

Javaid, Zeeshan, "Russia Agrees to Finance IP Gas Pipeline Project," *Daily Times*, June 28, 2012. As of July 17, 2012:
http://www.dailytimes.com.pk/default.asp?page=2012%5C06%5C28%5Cstory_28-6-2012_pg5_8

Javed, Bassam, "Indian Role in Afghanistan Spells Danger for Pakistan," *International News*, February 10, 2012. As of June 25, 2012:
http://www.thenews.com.pk/Todays-News-6-91998-Indian-role-in-Afghanistan-spells-danger-for-Pakistan

Joshi, Shashank, "India's Strategic Calculus in Afghanistan," *Foreign Policy*, October 6, 2011. As of June 15, 2012:
http://afpak.foreignpolicy.com/posts/2011/10/06/indias_strategic_calculus_in_afghanistan

Joshua, Anita, "Bickering Still on over NATO Lines," *The Hindu*, May 28, 2012. As of June 19, 2012:
http://www.thehindu.com/news/international/article3466626.ece

Kapila, Subhash, "Afghanistan: London Conference 2010 a Strategic Failure," South Asia Analysis Group, Paper 3643, February 2, 2010. As of June 19, 2012:
http://southasiaanalysis.org/%5Cpapers37%5Cpaper3643.html

Kaplan, Robert D., "Behind the Indian Embassy Bombing," *Atlantic*, August 2008. As of June 15, 2012:
http://www.theatlantic.com/magazine/archive/2008/08/behind-the-indian-embassy-bombing/6949/

Khan, Ijaz, *Pakistan's Strategic Culture and Foreign Policy Making: A Study of Pakistan's Post 9/11 Afghan Policy Change*, New York: Nova Science Publishers, 2007.

Khan, Ismail, "Prison Term for Helping C.I.A. Find bin Laden," *New York Times*, May 23, 2012. As of June 25, 2012:
http://www.nytimes.com/2012/05/24/world/asia/doctor-who-helped-find-bin-laden-given-jail-term-official-says.html

Khan, Riaz M., *Afghanistan and Pakistan: Conflict, Extremism, and Resistance to Modernity*, Washington, D.C.: Woodrow Wilson Center Press, 2011.

Khan, Simbal, "India's Planned Investment in Afghanistan," *Express Tribune*, September 9, 2011. As of June 15, 2012:
http://tribune.com.pk/story/248759/indias-planned-investment-in-afghanistan/

King, Laura, "Former Afghan President Burhanuddin Rabbani Assassinated," *Los Angeles Times*, September 20, 2011. As of June 18, 2012:
http://articles.latimes.com/2011/sep/20/world/la-fg-afghanistan-rabbani-20110921

Klapper, Bradley, and Rebecca Santana, "US Says Sorry, Pakistan Opens Afghan Supply Lines," Associated Press, July 3, 3012.

Krasner, Stephen D., "Talking Tough to Pakistan," *Foreign Affairs*, January–February 2012.

Kronstadt, K. Alan, *Pakistan–U.S. Relations*, Washington, D.C.: Congressional Research Service, R41832, May 24, 2012.

Kuchins, Andrew C., and Thomas M. Sanderson, *The Northern Distribution Network and Afghanistan: Geopolitical Challenges and Opportunities—A Report of the CSIS Transnational Threats Project and the Russia and Eurasia Program*, Washington, D.C.: Center for Strategic and International Studies, January 2010. As of June 19, 2012:
http://csis.org/files/publication/091229_Kuchins_NDNandAfghan_Web.pdf

Ladwig, Walter C. III, "India and Military Power Projection: Will the Land of Gandhi Become a Conventional Great Power?" *Asian Survey*, Vol. 50, No. 6, November–December 2010, pp. 1162–1183.

Lavoy, Peter R., "India in 2006: A New Emphasis on Engagement," *Asian Survey*, Vol. 47, No. 1, January–February 2007, pp. 113–124.

Levine, Adam, "Panetta Calls Insurgent Attacks in Afghanistan a 'Sign of Weakness,'" CNN, September 22, 2011. As of June 18, 2012:
http://articles.cnn.com/2011-09-22/us/us_mullen-security_1_haqqani-network-pakistan-s-inter-services-intelligence-kabul-attack

Lodhi, Iftikhar A., "Attack on the Indian Embassy in Kabul: Time to Sober Up," Singapore: Institute of South Asian Studies, Brief 75, July 15, 2008. As of June 19, 2012:
http://www.isas.nus.edu.sg/Attachments/PublisherAttachment/ISAS_Briefs_76pdf_22102009124134.pdf

Lynch, Colum, "India Threatens to Pull Plug on Peacekeeping," *Foreign Policy*, June 14, 2011. As of June 14, 2012:
http://turtlebay.foreignpolicy.com/posts/2011/06/14/india_threatens_to_pull_plug_on_peacekeeping

Malhotra, Jyoti, "Iran's Chabahar Port Eclipses Pakistan in Race for Afghan Profits," *Business Standard*, July 2, 2012. As of July 17, 2012:
http://www.business-standard.com/india/news/
iran%5Cs-chabahar-port-eclipses-pakistan-in-race-for-afghan-profits/479103/

Maley, William, "Afghanistan and Its Region," in J. Alexander Thier, ed., *The Future of Afghanistan*, Washington, D.C.: U.S. Institute of Peace, 2009, pp. 81–92.

Markey, Daniel, "A False Choice in Pakistan," *Foreign Affairs*, July–August 2007.

Masood, Salman, and Eric Schmitt, "Tensions Flare Between U.S. and Pakistan After Strike," *New York Times*, November 26, 2011. As of June 19, 2012:
http://www.nytimes.com/2011/11/27/world/asia/pakistan-says-nato-helicopters-kill-dozens-of-soldiers.html

Masood, Salman, and Declan Walsh, "Pakistan Gives U.S. a List of Demands, Including an End to C.I.A. Drone Strikes," *New York Times*, April 12, 2012. As of June 19, 2012:
http://www.nytimes.com/2012/04/13/world/asia/pakistan-demands-an-end-to-cia-drone-strikes.html

Mazzetti, Mark, and Dexter Filkins, "Secret Joint Raid Captures Taliban's Top Commander," *New York Times*, February 15, 2010. As of June 18, 2012:
http://www.nytimes.com/2010/02/16/world/asia/16intel.html

Mazzetti, Mark, and Eric Schmitt, "Pakistanis Aided Attack in Kabul, U.S. Officials Say," *New York Times*, August 1, 2008. As of June 18, 2012:
http://www.nytimes.com/2008/08/01/world/asia/01pstan.html

McChrystal, Stanley A., commander, International Security Assistance Force and U.S. Forces–Afghanistan, "COMISAF's Initial Assessment," memorandum to Secretary of Defense Robert M. Gates, August 30, 2009.

McGivering, Jill, "Afghan People 'Losing Confidence,'" BBC News, February 9, 2009. As of June 14, 2012:
http://news.bbc.co.uk/2/hi/south_asia/7872353.stm

Miglani, Sanjeev, "Indian Firms Eye Huge Mining Investment in Afghanistan," Reuters, September 14, 2011. As of June 15, 2012:
http://in.reuters.com/article/2011/09/14/idINIndia-59324720110914

Ministry of External Affairs, India, "Joint Declaration Between India and Afghanistan on the Occasion of the Visit of the Prime Minister of India," May 12, 2011. As of June 18, 2012:
http://www.mea.gov.in/mystart.php?id=100517624

Ministry of Finance, Islamic Republic of Afghanistan, *Donor Financial Review*, Report 1388, November 2009.

Mohan, C. Raja, "India and the Balance of Power," *Foreign Affairs*, July–August 2006.

———, "How Obama Can Get South Asia Right," *Washington Quarterly*, Vol. 32, No. 2, April 2009.

Mojumdar, Aunohita, "India's Role in Afghanistan: Narrow Vision Returns Meagre Gains," *Times of India*, April 17, 2010. As of June 19, 2012:
http://articles.timesofindia.indiatimes.com/2010-04-17/
india/28144375_1_indian-role-strategic-interests-foreign-policy

Moreau, Ron, and Sabrina Taversine, "The End of al Qaeda?" *Newsweek*, August 7, 2009.

Mukherjee, Pranab, external affairs minister, "India and the Global Balance of Power," address on the occasion of the national launch of the Global India Foundation, January 16, 2007a. As of June 15, 2012:
http://www.indianembassy.org.ua/english/speech7.htm

———, speech at the Research and Information System for Developing Countries and South Asia Centre for Policy Studies Conference, "Economic Cooperation in SAARC: SAFTA and Beyond," New Delhi, March 19, 2007b. As of June 15, 2012:
http://www.indianembassy.org/prdetail787/--%09--speech-by-the-external-affairs-minister,-mr.-pranab-mukherjee-at-the-ris-saceps-conference-of-andquot%3Beconomic-cooperation-in-saarc%3A-safta-and-beyondandquot%3B

Mukhopadhaya, Gautam, "India," in Ashley J. Tellis and Aroop Mukharji, eds., *Is a Regional Strategy Viable in Afghanistan?* Washington, D.C.: Carnegie Endowment for International Peace, 2010, pp. 27–38. As of June 14, 2012:
http://www.carnegieendowment.org/files/regional_approach.pdf

"Natural Gas Consumption Declines," *Pakistan Observer*, c. 2011. As of June 14, 2012:
http://pakobserver.net/detailnews.asp?id=100263

Nayak, Debiprasad, and Biman Mukherji, "Tehran Sets Trade Deals with India Amid Curbs," *Wall Street Journal*, May 9, 2012.

Nelson, Dean, "India Plans 'World's Most Dangerous Railroad' from Afghanistan to Iran," *Telegraph*, November 2, 2011. As of June 15, 2012:
http://www.telegraph.co.uk/news/worldnews/asia/india/8862583/
India-plans-worlds-most-dangerous-railroad-from-Afghanistan-to-Iran.html

Nyrop, Richard F., and Donald M. Seekins, eds., *Afghanistan: A Country Study*, Washington, D.C.: Federal Research Division, Library of Congress, January 1986. As of June 18, 2012:
http://purl.access.gpo.gov/GPO/LPS18505

Obama, Barack, remarks on a new strategy for Afghanistan and Pakistan, Washington, D.C., March 27, 2009. As of June 19, 2012:
http://www.whitehouse.gov/the-press-office/remarks-president-a-new-strategy-afghanistan-and-pakistan

———, "Remarks of President Barack Obama on the Way Forward in Afghanistan," Washington, D.C.: White House, June 22, 2011. As of June 18, 2012:
http://kabul.usembassy.gov/obama-speech.html

"Obama Appreciates India's Role in Afghanistan," *The Hindu*, November 7, 2010. As of June 15, 2012:
http://www.thehindu.com/news/national/article872842.ece

Office of the Special Representative for Afghanistan and Pakistan, U.S. Department of State, *Afghanistan and Pakistan Regional Stabilization Strategy*, Washington, D.C., updated February 2010. As of June 18, 2012:
http://www.state.gov/documents/organization/135728.pdf

Pai, Nitin, and Rohit Pradhan, "Why India Must Send Troops to Afghanistan," *Pragati: The Indian National Interest Review*, January 1, 2010. As of June 19, 2012:
http://pragati.nationalinterest.in/2010/01/why-india-must-send-troops-to-afghanistan/

"Pak Assures Iran on Gas Pipeline Project," Press Trust of India, February 16, 2012.

"Pakistan," *World Factbook*, Washington, D.C.: Central Intelligence Agency, last updated June 7, 2012. As of June 18, 2012:
https://www.cia.gov/library/publications/the-world-factbook/geos/pk.html

"Pakistan 'Backed Haqqani Attack on Kabul'—Mike Mullen," BBC News, September 22, 2011. As of June 25, 2012:
http://www.bbc.co.uk/news/world-us-canada-15024344

"Pakistan Consumes Half of Its Gas Reserves," *Daily Times*, December 28, 2011. As of June 14, 2012:
http://www.dailytimes.com.pk/default.asp?page=2011%5C12%5C28%5Cstory_28-12-2011_pg5_10

"Pakistan Oil and Gas Report Q4 2011," *Business Monitor International*, September 16, 2011.

"Pakistan Our Twin Brother, India a Great Friend: Hamid Karzai," *Times of India*, October 5, 2011. As of June 18, 2012:
http://timesofindia.indiatimes.com/india/Pakistan-our-twin-brother-India-a-great-friend-Hamid-Karzai/
articleshow/10246454.cms

"Pakistan to Boycott Key Meeting on Afghanistan," *Associated Press*, November 29, 2011.

Pant, Harsh V., "India in Afghanistan: A Test Case for a Rising Power," *Contemporary South Asia*, Vol. 18, No. 2, 2010a, pp. 133–153.

——, *India's Challenge in Afghanistan: With Power Comes Responsibility*, Philadelphia, Pa.: Center for the Advanced Study of India, Working Paper 10-02, March 2010b.

——, "India's Changing Role: The Afghanistan Conflict," *Middle East Quarterly*, Vol. 18, No. 2, Spring 2011, pp. 31–39. As of June 15, 2012:
http://www.meforum.org/2895/india-afghanistan

Patil, Pratibha Devisingh, president of India, speech at the banquet in honor of the president of the Islamic Republic of Afghanistan, Hamid Karzai, New Delhi, August 4, 2008. As of June 15, 2012:
http://presidentofindia.nic.in/bqsp040808.html

Pattanaik, Smruti S., "India in Afghanistan: Engagement Without Strategy," *ISDA Comment*, January 28, 2011. As of June 15, 2012:
http://www.idsa.in/?q=node/6621/2158

Philip, Catherine, "Pervez Musharraf Was Playing 'Double Game' with U.S.," *Times*, February 17, 2009.

Ploch, Lauren, Christopher M. Blanchard, Ronald O'Rourke, R. Chuck Mason, and Rawle O. King, *Piracy Off the Horn of Africa*, Washington, D.C.: Congressional Research Service, R40528, April 27, 2011. As of June 14, 2012:
http://www.fas.org/sgp/crs/row/R40528.pdf

Polgreen, Lydia, "Karzai Tries to Soothe Pakistan over Warmer Relations with India," *New York Times*, October 5, 2011. As of June 18, 2012:
http://www.nytimes.com/2011/10/06/world/asia/
karzai-tries-to-soothe-pakistan-over-warmer-relations-with-india.html

Polgreen, Lydia, and Souad Mekhennet, "Militant Network Is Intact Long After Mumbai Siege," *New York Times*, September 29, 2009. As of June 14, 2012:
http://www.nytimes.com/2009/09/30/world/asia/30mumbai.html?pagewanted=all

Poullada, Leon B., "Afghanistan and the United States: The Crucial Years," *Middle East Journal*, Vol. 35, No. 2, Spring 1981, pp. 178–190.

Pubby, Manu, "50 Afghan Cadets Train at IMA," *Indian Express*, July 22, 2011. As of June 15, 2012:
http://www.indianexpress.com/news/50-afghan-cadets-train-at-ima/820715/

Pyatt, Geoffrey, principal deputy assistant secretary, Bureau of South and Central Asian Affairs, U.S. Department of State, "Next Steps on the Silk Road," remarks to members of the Federation of Indian Chambers of Commerce and Industry, Chennai, November 15, 2011. As of June 15, 2012:
http://newdelhi.usembassy.gov/sr111115.html

Quinn, Andrew, "U.S. Keeps India Waiting on Iran Sanctions Waiver," *Reuters*, May 7, 2012. As of June 19, 2012:
http://in.reuters.com/article/2012/05/07/usa-iran-india-idINDEE84603720120507

Rabasa, Angel, Robert D. Blackwill, Peter Chalk, Kim Cragin, C. Christine Fair, Brian A. Jackson, Brian Michael Jenkins, Seth G. Jones, Nathaniel Shestak, and Ashley J. Tellis, *The Lessons of Mumbai*, Santa Monica, Calif.: RAND Corporation, OP-249-RC, 2009. As of June 14, 2012:
http://www.rand.org/pubs/occasional_papers/OP249.html

Rahimullah, Yousafzai, "Pakistan's Loss in Afghanistan Is India's Gain," *News*, July 13, 2003.

Ramachandran, Sudha, "India Takes a Slow Road," *Asia Times*, January 27, 2007. As of June 15, 2012:
http://www.atimes.com/atimes/South_Asia/IA27Df04.html

Rao, Nirupama, foreign secretary, speech at the French Institute of International Relations, Paris, May 5, 2011. As of June 15, 2012:
http://amb-inde.fr/fr/component/content/article/282-transcript-of-foreign-secretary-smt-nirupama-raos-speech-at-the-french-institute-of-international-relations-ifri-paris-may-5-2011

Rashid, Ahmed, "The Taliban: Exporting Extremism," *Foreign Affairs*, Vol. 78, No. 6, November–December 1999, pp. 22–35.

———, *Taliban: Islam, Oil and the New Great Game in Central Asia*, London: I. B. Tauris, 2000.

———, *Taliban: Militant Islam, Oil and Fundamentalism in Central Asia*, New Haven, Conn.: Yale University Press, 2010.

"RAW Active in Indian Consulates: Pakistan," *Dawn*, August 2, 2003. As of June 15, 2012:
http://archives.dawn.com/2003/08/02/top12.htm

Rehman, Sherry, "Ambassador Rehman's Speech at the United States Institute of Peace (USIP)," Washington, D.C., February 15, 2012. As of June 14, 2012:
http://www.embassyofpakistanusa.org/news500_02152012.php

Rivera, Ray, and Sangar Rahimi, "Afghan President Says His Country Would Back Pakistan in a Clash with the U.S.," *New York Times*, October 23, 2011. As of June 18, 2012:
http://www.nytimes.com/2011/10/24/world/asia/
karzai-says-afghanistan-would-back-pakistan-in-a-conflict-with-us.html

Rizvi, Hasan-Askari, *Pakistan's Foreign Policy: An Overview 1947–2004*, Pakistan Institute of Legislative Development and Transparency, Briefing Paper 11, April 2004. As of June 18, 2012:
http://millat.com/democracy/Foreign%20Policy/Briefing_Paper_english_11.pdf

Roche, Elizabeth, "India, Pakistan's 'Proxy War' in Afghanistan," Agence France-Presse, March 3, 2010.

Rodriguez, Alex, and Mark Magnier, "Pakistan, India Take Another Cautious Step Forward," *Los Angeles Times*, November 7, 2011. As of June 18, 2012:
http://articles.latimes.com/2011/nov/07/world/la-fg-india-pakistan-trade-20111107

Roy, Meena Singh, "Pakistan's Strategies in Central Asia," *Strategic Analysis*, Vol. 30, No. 4, October–December 2006, pp. 798–833.

Rubin, Alissa, "Militant Group Expands Attacks in Afghanistan," *New York Times*, June 15, 2010. As of June 18, 2012:
http://www.nytimes.com/2010/06/16/world/asia/16lashkar.html

Rubin, Barnett R., *The Fragmentation of Afghanistan: State Formation and Collapse in the International System*, New Haven, Conn.: Yale University Press, 2002.

Ruttig, Thomas, "The Taliban Arrest Wave in Pakistan: Reasserting Strategic Depth?" *CTC Sentinel*, Vol. 3, No. 3, March 2010, pp. 5–7. As of June 18, 2012:
http://www.ctc.usma.edu/wp-content/uploads/2010/08/CTCSentinel-Vol3Iss3-art2.pdf

Sahgal, Arun, "U.S. Af-Pak Strategy and Afghanistan's Alternative Futures: Options for India," in R. K. Sawhney, Arun Sahgal, and Gurmeet Kanwal, eds., *Afghanistan: A Role for India*, New Delhi: Centre for Land Warfare Studies, 2011.

Salahuddin, Sayed, "Karzai Says Pakistan Behind Indian Embassy Bomb," Reuters, July 14, 2008. As of June 18, 2012:
http://in.reuters.com/article/2008/07/14/idINIndia-34507520080714

Sawhney, R. K., "Afghanistan Today," in R. K. Sawhney, Arun Sahgal, and Gurmeet Kanwal, eds., *Afghanistan: A Role for India*, New Delhi: Centre for Land Warfare Studies, 2011, pp. 1–20.

Schaffer, Teresita C., *India and the United States in the 21st Century: Reinventing Partnership*, Washington, D.C.: Center for Strategic and International Studies Press, 2009.

Schreck, Adam, and Chris Brummitt, "Iran Looks to Boost Energy Ties to Nearby Pakistan," Associated Press, March 1, 2012.

Sen, Nirupam, Permanent Representative from India to the United Nations, statement on the situation in Afghanistan to the United Nations Security Council, July 9, 2008. As of June 14, 2012:
http://www.un.int/india/2008/ind1436.pdf

Shah, Pir Zubair, and Carlotta Gall, "For Pakistan, Deep Ties to Militant Network May Trump U.S. Pressure," *New York Times*, October 31, 2011. As of June 18, 2012: http://www.nytimes.com/2011/11/01/world/asia/haqqani-militants-act-like-pakistans-protected-partners.html

Shahid, Shiza, *Engaging Regional Players in Afghanistan*, Washington, D.C.: Center for Strategic and International Studies, November 24, 2009. As of June 15, 2012: http://csis.org/publication/engaging-regional-players-afghanistan

Sharma, Raghav, *India and Afghanistan: Charting the Future*, New Delhi: Institute of Peace and Conflict Studies, Special Report 69, April 2009. As of June 14, 2012: http://www.ipcs.org/pdf_file/issue/SR69-Final.pdf

Shashikumar, V. K., "Indian Built Zaranj–Delaram Highway Under Taliban Control," *Indian Defence Review*, October 1, 2011. As of June 15, 2012: http://www.indiandefencereview.com/news/indian-built-zaranj-delaram-highway-under-taliban-control/

Singh, Sushant K., "A Bigger Military Presence Is Essential If India Is to Shape Afghanistan's Future," *Pragati: The Indian National Interest Review*, No. 17, August 2008, pp. 12–13. As of June 18, 2012: http://pragati.nationalinterest.in/wp-content/uploads/2008/08/pragati-issue17-aug2008-communityed.pdf

Sinnott, Peter, "Peeling the Waziristan Onion: Central Asians in Armed Islamist Movements in Afghanistan and Pakistan," *China and Eurasia Forum Quarterly*, Vol. 7, No. 4, 2009, pp. 33–53. As of June 18, 2012: http://www.chinaeurasia.org/images/stories/isdp-cefq/CEFQ200912/cefq7.4ps33-53.pdf

Stern, Jessica, "Pakistan's Jihad Culture," *Foreign Affairs*, November–December 2000.

Subrahmanyam, K., "War in Afghanistan," New Delhi: National Maritime Foundation, September 6, 2009.

"Support for U.S. Efforts Plummets Amid Afghanistan's Ongoing Strife," ABC News/BBC/ARD poll, February 9, 2009. As of June 15, 2012: http://abcnews.go.com/images/PollingUnit/1083a1Afghanistan2009.pdf

Tadjbakhsh, Shahrbanou, *South Asia and Afghanistan: The Robust India-Pakistan Rivalry*, Oslo: Peace Research Institute Oslo, 2011.

"Taliban Flags Start to Spring Fighting Season," Associated Press, May 2, 2011.

Tankel, Stephen, *Lashkar-e-Taiba: From 9/11 to Mumbai*, London: International Centre for the Study of Radicalisation and Political Violence, April–May 2009. As of June 18, 2012: http://icsr.info/news/attachments/1240846916ICSRTankelReport.pdf

Tariq, Mohammed Osman, Najla Ayoubi, and Fazel Rabi Haqbeen, *Afghanistan in 2011: A Survey of the Afghan People*, Kabul: Asia Foundation, 2011. As of June 15, 2012: http://asiafoundation.org/resources/pdfs/TAF2011AGSurvey.pdf

Tavernise, Sabrina, and Abdul Waheed Wafa, "17 Die in Kabul Bomb Attack," *New York Times*, October 8, 2009. As of June 18, 2012: http://www.nytimes.com/2009/10/09/world/asia/09afghan.html

Tellis, Ashley J., "The Merits of Dehyphenation: Explaining U.S. Success in Engaging India and Pakistan," *Washington Quarterly*, Vol. 31, No. 4, Autumn 2008, pp. 21–42.

———, "Implementing a Regional Approach to Afghanistan: Multiple Alternatives, Modest Possibilities," in Ashley J. Tellis and Aroop Mukharji, eds., *Is a Regional Strategy Viable in Afghanistan?* Washington, D.C.: Carnegie Endowment for International Peace, 2010, pp. 85–126. As of June 14, 2012: http://www.carnegieendowment.org/files/regional_approach.pdf

———, "Creating New Facts on the Ground: Why the Diplomatic Surge Cannot Yet Produce a Regional Solution in Afghanistan," Washington, D.C.: Carnegie Endowment for International Peace, Policy Brief 91, May 2011. As of June 15, 2012: http://carnegieendowment.org/files/afghan_policy.pdf

Tharoor, Ishaan, "India, Pakistan and the Battle for Afghanistan," *Time*, December 5, 2009. As of June 15, 2012: http://www.time.com/time/world/article/0,8599,1945666,00.html

———, "The Bonn Conference: Can Afghanistan Be Saved Without Pakistan on Board?" *Time*, December 5, 2011. As of June 18, 2012:
http://world.time.com/2011/12/05/the-bonn-conference-can-afghanistan-be-saved-without-pakistan-on-board/

Tharoor, Shashi, "Hooray for Bollywood: India's 'Soft Power,'" *Taipei Times*, January 7, 2008. As of June 15, 2012:
http://www.taipeitimes.com/News/editorials/archives/2008/01/07/2003396110

Transparency International, *Corruption Perceptions Index 2011*, 2011. As of June 18, 2012:
http://transparency.org/whatwedo/pub/corruption_perceptions_index_2011

"Turkmenistan-Afghanistan-Pakistan-India Gas Pipeline: South Asia's Key Project," *PetroMin Pipeliner*, April–June 2011. As of June 14, 2012:
http://www.pm-pipeliner.safan.com/mag/ppl0411/r06.pdf

"U.S. AfPak Envoy Backs Indian Investment in Afghanistan, Strategic Pact," Indo Asian News Service, October 12, 2011.

U.S. Agency for International Development, "Energy in Pakistan," working paper, April 2011a. As of June 19, 2012:
http://transition.usaid.gov/pk/docs/sectors/Energy_Working_Paper.pdf

———, "Pakistan: Energy Program," September 2011b. As of June 19, 2012:
http://transition.usaid.gov/pk/sectors/energy/docs/en_factsheet.pdf

U.S. Department of State, "U.S.–India Strategic Dialogue Joint Statement," media note, June 3, 2010. As of June 18, 2012:
http://www.state.gov/r/pa/prs/ps/2010/06/142645.htm

U.S. Energy Information Administration, "Pakistan: Country Analysis Brief," June 30, 2010a.

———, "India: Country Analysis Brief," August 2010b.

———, "India," Washington, D.C., Country Analysis Brief, November 21, 2011. As of June 19, 2012:
http://www.eia.gov/EMEU/cabs/India/pdf.pdf

"U.S. Set to Ignore Pakistan, Afghanistan in Taliban Talks," *Press TV*, February 10, 2012. As of June 18, 2012:
http://www.presstv.ir/detail/226023.html

"U.S. Suspends $800 Million in Aid to Pakistan," NPR, July 10, 2011. As of June 14, 2012:
http://www.npr.org/2011/07/10/137746664/u-s-to-suspend-800-million-in-aid-to-pakistan

Verma, Arjun, and Teresita Schaffer, "A Difficult Road Ahead: India's Policy on Afghanistan," *South Asia Monitor*, No. 144, August 1, 2010. As of June 15, 2012:
http://csis.org/files/publication/SAM_144.pdf

Wafa, Abdul Waheed, and Alan Cowell, "Suicide Car Blast Kills 41 in Afghan Capital," *New York Times*, July 8, 2008. As of June 18, 2012:
http://www.nytimes.com/2008/07/08/world/asia/08afghanistan.html

Waldman, Matt, *The Sun in the Sky: The Relationship Between Pakistan's ISI and Afghan Insurgents*, London: London School of Economics and Political Science, Crisis States Research Centre, Working Paper 18, 2010.

Warrick, Joby, and Karen DeYoung, "CIA Helped India, Pakistan Share Secrets in Probe of Mumbai Siege," *Washington Post*, February 16, 2009. As of June 25, 2012:
http://www.washingtonpost.com/wp-dyn/content/article/2009/02/15/AR2009021501957.html

Waslekar, Sundeep, Leena Pillai, and Shabnam Siddiqui, *The Future of Pakistan*, Mumbai: Strategic Foresight Group, 2002.

Wax, Emily, "India's Eager Courtship of Afghanistan Comes at a Steep Price," *Washington Post*, April 3, 2010. As of June 15, 2012:
http://www.washingtonpost.com/wp-dyn/content/article/2010/04/02/AR2010040204313.html

"We Have Only Four Consulates in Afghanistan, Exactly the Same Number We Had Earlier," *Rediff News*, February 26, 2009. As of June 15, 2012:
http://specials.rediff.com/news/2009/feb/26sld5-interview-with-indias-afghan-envoy-jayant-prasad.htm

Weinbaum, Marvin G., and Jonathan B. Harder, "Pakistan's Afghan Policies and Their Consequences," *Contemporary South Asia*, Vol. 16, No. 1, 2008, pp. 25–38.

Weinbaum, Marvin G., and Haseeb Humayoon, "The Intertwined Destinies of Afghanistan and Pakistan," in J. Alexander Thier, ed., *The Future of Afghanistan*, Washington, D.C.: U.S. Institute of Peace, 2009, pp. 93–104.

"What Is Bollywood?" *Newsround*, undated. As of June 15, 2012:
http://news.bbc.co.uk/cbbcnews/hi/find_out/guides/2003/bollywood/newsid_2683000/2683799.stm

White House, "Joint Statement by President Obama and Prime Minister Singh of India," press release, November 8, 2010. As of June 18, 2012:
http://www.whitehouse.gov/the-press-office/2010/11/08/
joint-statement-president-obama-and-prime-minister-singh-india

"White Paper of the Interagency Policy Group's Report on U.S. Policy Toward Afghanistan and Pakistan," undated. As of June 18, 2012:
http://www.whitehouse.gov/assets/documents/Afghanistan-Pakistan_White_Paper.pdf

Yardley, Jim, "Indians Host Clinton While Also Wooing Iran," *New York Times*, May 8, 2012. As of June 19, 2012:
http://www.nytimes.com/2012/05/09/world/asia/
india-and-iran-keep-economic-relations-despite-us-nudge.html?pagewanted=all

Younossi, Obaid, Peter Dahl Thruelsen, Jonathan Vaccaro, Jerry M. Sollinger, and Brian Grady, *The Long March: Building an Afghan National Army*, Santa Monica, Calif.: RAND Corporation, MG-845-RDCC/OSD, 2009. As of June 18, 2012:
http://www.rand.org/pubs/monographs/MG845.html

Zoellick, Robert B., "Afghanistan's Biggest Need: A Flourishing Economy," *Washington Post*, July 22, 2011. As of June 18, 2012:
http://www.washingtonpost.com/opinions/afghanistans-biggest-need-a-flourishing-economy/2011/07/19/gIQAGNMIUI_story.html